Advance praise for *Legacy of Love*

"*Legacy of Love* is replete with concrete, practical family advice based on Kimberly Hahn's personal experience through the various stages of being a wife and mother. The text is heavily spiced with Scripture, drawing relevance from ancient wisdom to help us become wise families in the modern world."

—Father Mitch Pacwa, s.j.

"*Legacy of Love* is what I will hand parents who need help and encouragement with their growing families. Raising children today takes more than a village; it takes a family rooted in the Church. Kimberly Hahn has put together an understandable and doable master plan for successful families."

—Jeff Cavins, president of The Great Adventure
Bible Study System

"*Legacy of Love* is a must-have resource for families in today's media-saturated world. It's jam-packed with practical advice based on the timeless truths of Scripture and the teachings of the Church and filled with wisdom and experience spoken from Kimberly's humble heart."

—Teresa Tomeo, syndicated Catholic talk-show host
and bestselling Catholic author

"As a parent of five teens, I found Kimberly Hahn's latest work, *Legacy of Love: Biblical Wisdom for Parenting Teens and Young Adults,* very encouraging and helpful. We are living in an age when raising godly young men and women is very difficult. As parents we are competing with many voices, all which seem contrary to raising our children with biblical values and godly standards. Kimberly's knowledge and insights are refreshing for weary parents, and the wisdom she shares is timeless."

—Michaelann Martin, author, speaker, and mother of eight

LEGACY OF LOVE

LEGACY
OF
LOVE

BIBLICAL
WISDOM
FOR
PARENTING
TEENS
AND
YOUNG
ADULTS

Kimberly Hahn

SERVANT
BOOKS

PUBLISHED BY ST. ANTHONY MESSENGER PRESS
CINCINNATI, OHIO

Unless otherwise noted, Scripture passages have been taken from the *Revised Standard Version*, Catholic edition. Copyright 1946, 1952, 1971 by the Division of Christian Education of the National Council of Churches of Christ in the USA. Used by permission. All rights reserved.

Quotes are taken from the English translation of the *Catechism of the Catholic Church* for the United States of America (indicated as *CCC*), 2nd ed. Copyright 1997 by United States Catholic Conference—Libreria Editrice Vaticana.

Cover design by Connie Wolfer
Cover image © The Metropolitan Museum of Art / Art Resource, NY
Juan de Flandes , *The Marriage Feast at Cana*
Book design by Mark Sullivan

LIBRARY OF CONGRESS CATALOGING-IN-PUBLICATION DATA
Hahn, Kimberly.
Legacy of love : Biblical wisdom for parenting teens and young adults / Kimberly Hahn.
p. cm. — (Life-nurturing love)
Includes bibliographical references.
ISBN 978-1-61636-000-9 (alk. paper)
1. Motherhood—Religious aspects—Catholic Church. 2. Parent and teenager—Religious aspects—Catholic Church. 3. Parent and adult child—Religious aspects—Catholic Church. 4. Catholic teenagers—Religious life. 5. Young adults—Religious life. 6. Bible. O.T. Proverbs XXXI, 10-31—Criticism, interpretation, etc. I. Title.
BX2353.H25 2011
248.8'431088282—dc22
2011013238

ISBN 978-1-61636-000-9

Published by Servant Books, an imprint of St. Anthony Messenger Press.
28 W. Liberty St.
Cincinnati, OH 45202
www.AmericanCatholic.org
www.ServantBooks.org

Printed in the United States of America.
Printed on acid-free paper.
11 12 13 14 15   5 4 3 2 1

To my sons, the men of God for whom I prayed:

*To **Michael,** my firstborn, for the wonderful ways you have been responsible as our point man, caring for your younger siblings, sharing in the joy of their births, and offering words of wisdom.*

*To **Gabriel,** man of God's strength, for the joy you bring through your playfulness, the intensity of commitment you inspire, and your sensitive spirit.*

*To **Jeremiah,** my young gentleman, for the peace you bring through contentment, the joy you bring as the family secret keeper, and the ways you bridge the younger and older kids in the family.*

*To **Joseph,** my combo kid, for the strengths you draw from each of your older siblings in a mix all your own, the humor you use to diffuse tension, and the compassion you communicate to family and friends.*

*To **David,** my youngest, for the passion you bring to life, the faith, the piano, and the soccer field; for your sense of humor and tender affection.*

Contents

Introduction

Welcome to the fourth installment of the *Life-Nurturing Love* series, based on Proverbs 31:10–31. In this series we have discussed many ways the Proverbs 31 woman does good for her husband through her care for their household and home. She is diligent in her faith and in her actions. Consequently her family flourishes, her husband enjoys a good reputation, and her household is well managed.

In this book you will explore more about parenting, focusing on teens and young adults, and about extending your faith in action beyond your homes. How do you transition from a nuclear family to an extended family as your children marry and establish families of their own? How do your married children and their families remain a part of your larger family while growing increasingly independent? And how do you lead—and reach beyond—your family to witness to your parish, your neighborhood, your country, and your world?

PRIORITY LIVING

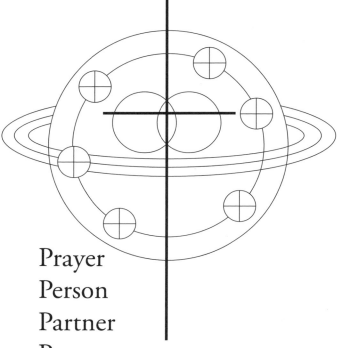

Prayer
Person
Partner
Parent
Provider
Periphery

- *Parents and family members*
- *Parish and neighbors*
- *Policies for state and nation*
- *Proclaim the Good News*

Here is a brief explanation of the illustration "Priority Living." The cross in the center stands for your relationship with the Lord, your primary priority. The two entwined circles represent who you are as a daughter of God, created and redeemed by him, and your relationship with your spouse. The cross in the center of your joined circles reminds you to keep Christ in the center of your marriage.

The next priority is your family circle. The larger line connecting the little circles that surround the entwined circles represents your relationships with your children. The circle encasing the little circles represents how you provide for your family's needs, the tasks that nurture your family toward a culture of life and love.

Finally, the horizontal rings encircling the nucleus are your peripheral priorities. They are genuine priorities that have a place in your life, though they are secondary to your primary call to your family.

This study may trigger thoughts about your life as a teen, your children who will be teens, or your children who are currently teenagers. You may be anticipating a relationship with a son- or daughter-in-law, or you may already have one. You may think about your grandparents and ways you want to imitate them. Or you may want a different vision for grandparenting than you experienced from either your grandparents or your parents as they grandparented your children. Can you offer more?

No matter where you are coming from, this is a *new beginning*. Take what you have been given and build on it. My prayer is that you will be inspired to serve the Lord and your family in new ways. I hope you will not feel overwhelmed by too many ideas.

We filmed the *Life-Nurturing Love* series so that you could share this study. In the back of each of the four books are copies of the outlines that correspond to the DVDs. You can enlarge and duplicate them and invite a few friends over to share this study. You can watch the DVDs as six studies or divide each talk in half and view the studies over twelve weeks. Encourage each woman to have her own copy of the book, since the book has much more material than the DVDs.

One part of the *Life-Nurturing Love* study is the material that you read or hear. Another is the women's small-group discussion, preferably intergenerational, where you share ideas about how to live this vocation more richly. Questions are included in Appendix B.

I want to thank the small-group leaders who facilitated this study when we filmed it at Franciscan University: Marianne DuBois, Amy McManamon, Julie Robbins, Laurie Traglia, Stacy Mitch, Pat Decker, Shelagh Pruni, Kathy McQuaig, Suzanne Heaps, Danielle Chodorowski, Martha Duff, and my mom, Patty Kirk. Many thanks to Kathy McQuaig for her indispensable editing.

Special thanks to Mary Collar and her husband, who paid for the filming, and the Cincinnati ladies from Mary's study, who prayed for this project and participated in the filming. Finally, extra special thanks to my beloved Scott, who for decades has encouraged me in my teaching and in our living this material.

PART ONE

She Opens Her Hand

to the Poor

—Proverbs 31:20

CHAPTER ONE

Personal Compassion for the Poor

The Proverbs 31 woman is as diligent in charity as she is in her work. She is intent to give and not simply determined to acquire. She lives the principle Jesus taught his disciples, "Every one to whom much is given, of him will much be required" (Luke 12:48).

Proverbs 31:20 reads, "She opens her hand to the poor, and reaches out her hands to the needy." She embraces the virtue of generosity in a personal way. She offers "the helpfulness of a sister's love, the tenderness of a mother's solicitude, [and] the awakening touch of a daughter's care."[1]

This is not pity; pity becomes mere sentimentality. This is *charity*. She offers compassionate love in action when necessary, not when it is convenient; true charity is rarely convenient. More than writing a check or offering a prayer, she serves the poor herself, caring for their specific needs. *She* opens her hand; *she* reaches out.

TIMELESS PERSPECTIVE

The Proverbs 31 woman knows—as do we—that earthly life is not all there is. She offers timely help from a timeless perspective. "Kindness is like a garden of blessings, and almsgiving endures for ever" (Sirach 40:17). Like the Proverbs 31 woman, we must balance prudent living and generous hearts.

If we are pilgrims on a journey, we should travel light. "Do not lay up for yourselves treasures on earth, where moth and rust consume and where thieves break in and steal, but lay up for yourselves treasures in heaven, where neither moth nor rust consumes and where thieves do not break in and steal. For where your treasure is, there will your heart be also" (Matthew 6:19–21). We cannot take our money with us, but we can honor the Lord by using it wisely. We do not give money or possessions as a substitute for more personal involvement but as an extension of ourselves.

Giving is an expression of faith, trusting God to provide for our needs. "Honor the LORD with your substance and with the first fruits of all your produce; then your barns will be filled with plenty, and your vats will be bursting with wine" (Proverbs 3:9–10). Today too many of us delay giving until we have enough money to spare. But how much is enough?

Giving is an act of worship. "On the first day of every week, each of you is to put something aside and store it up, as he may prosper, so that contributions need not be made when I come" (1 Corinthians 16:2). The early Christians established this pattern for us. Our Sunday offerings represent offering ourselves to the Lord.

Giving is an expression of gratitude. St. John Chrysostom taught, "[God] gives some people more than they need, not that they can enjoy great luxury, but to make them stewards of his bounty on behalf of orphans, the sick, and the crippled. If they are bad stewards, keeping this bounty to themselves, they will become poor in spirit, and their hearts will fill with misery. If they are good stewards, they will become rich in spirit, their hearts filling with joy."[2]

We have been blessed in order to be a blessing; in giving we will be blessed further. "He who has a bountiful eye will be blessed, for he shares his bread with the poor" (Proverbs 22:9; see Deuteronomy 15:10–11).

Giving is a matter of obedience. Tithing (giving the first 10 percent of our earnings to the Lord) is the beginning of Christian giving; almsgiving is giving beyond the tithe. Jesus said, "*When* you give alms,... *when* you pray,... *when* you fast..." (Matthew 6:3, 5, 16, emphasis mine). He assumes we will do these things. He promises, "Give, and it will be given to you; good measure, pressed down, shaken together, running over, will be put into your lap. For the measure you give will be the measure you get back" (Luke 6:38).

We cannot outgive God. As the author of Proverbs writes,

> One man gives freely, yet grows all the richer;
>> another withholds what he should give, and only suffers
> want.
> A liberal man will be enriched,
>> and one who waters will himself be watered.
> ...
> He who trusts in his riches will wither,
>> but the righteous will flourish like a green leaf.
> (Proverbs 11:24–25, 28)

If we refuse to be generous, we will incur judgment. The prophet Ezekiel declares that God's judgment on the citizens of Sodom was due in part to the people's lack of care for the poor: "Behold, this was the guilt of your sister Sodom; she and her daughters had pride, surfeit of food, and prosperous ease, but did not aid the poor and needy" (Ezekiel 16:49).

ACTS OF CHARITY ARE POWERFUL IN OUR LIVES

God does not require us to give for his sake; he requires us to give for our sake.

Acts of charity empower our prayers. In Isaiah's time people fasted and prayed, but their prayers went unanswered because of their lack of charity.

> Is not this the fast that I choose:
>> to loose the bonds of wickedness,
>> to undo the thongs of the yoke,
> to let the oppressed go free,
>> and to break every yoke?
> Is it not to share your bread with the hungry,
>> and bring the homeless poor into your house;
> when you see the naked, to cover him,
>> and not to hide yourself from your own flesh?
> Then shall your light break forth like the dawn,
>> and your healing shall spring up speedily;
> your righteousness shall go before you,
>> the glory of the Lord shall be your rear guard.
> Then you shall call, and the Lord will answer;
>> you shall cry, and he will say, Here I am. (Isaiah 58:6–9a)

When we care for those in need, God cares for our needs and answers our prayers.

Acts of charity weaken the power of money over us. Money itself is not evil, but the love of money, St. Paul warns, is the root of all evil (see 1 Timothy 6:6–10). We guard our hearts against avarice or greed through detachment: All we have comes from God, and we must be good stewards of it.

Acts of charity even become our response to enemies. When we show kindness to someone who has hurt us, we protect our hearts from sin while we consign him or her to God. "If your enemy is hungry, give him bread to eat; and if he is thirsty, give him water to drink; for you will heap coals of fire on his head, and the LORD will reward you" (Proverbs 25:21–22). In Jesus' name we help all, whether friend or foe, leaving the results to God.

WE PRAY TO BE AWARE OF OTHERS' NEEDS

Open our eyes to the needs of the poor. Jesus' summary of the law includes not only the command to love God with everything but also a second command—to love our neighbor as ourselves (see Matthew 22:37–40). Jesus makes it clear that our love for God is inseparably joined to our love of neighbor. We cannot simply say we do not see others' needs. "He who gives to the poor will not want, but he who hides his eyes will get many a curse" (Proverbs 28:27).

Open our ears to the cries of the poor. "Incline your ear to the poor, and answer him peaceably and gently" (Sirach 4:8). Otherwise, "he who closes his ear to the cry of the poor will himself cry out and not be heard" (Proverbs 21:13).

Open our hearts to the poor. We give as if giving to the Lord. "He who is kind to the poor lends to the LORD, and he will repay him for his deed" (Proverbs 19:17). What an awesome thought! If we lend to the poor, the person "indebted" to us is not the poor but God himself.

GENEROSITY ACCORDING TO PRIORITIES

Sometimes we are most generous to those farthest from us. We can more easily give an anonymous donation than meet practical needs in our family or parish. While generous to all, we must maintain our priorities: first, our family; second, the household of faith; third, the sojourner, the fatherless, and the widow; and fourth, the poor of our society. Our discernment comes through prayer and thoughtful reflection.

Family first. We must care for the needy people in our extended family. "If a widow has children or grandchildren, let them first learn their religious duty to their own family and make some return to their parents, for this is acceptable in the sight of God.... If any one does not provide for his relatives, and especially for his own family, he has disowned the faith and is worse than an unbeliever" (1 Timothy 5:4, 8).

These are very strong words. If we fail to provide for our own families, we have disowned the faith! Our top priority, after our nuclear family, is our extended family.

Household of faith, second. Our care extends next to the household of faith. "So then, as we have opportunity, let us do good to all men, and especially to those who are of the household of faith" (Galatians 6:10). As Pope Benedict XVI says, "Within the community of believers there can never be room for a poverty that denies anyone what is needed for a dignified life," for social service is "a well-ordered love of neighbour."[3]

St. James pointedly challenges us to love our fellow believers by caring for their practical needs. "If a brother or sister is poorly clothed and in lack of daily food, and one of you says to them, 'Go in peace, be warmed and filled,' without giving them the things needed for the body, what does it profit?" (James 2:15–16).

What about our spiritual fathers—our priests—who have embraced poverty to serve us? They are certainly part of the household of faith. What are their needs, and can we assist them? Are there household items we can fix or replace for them? Can we offer them a place to relax or vacation? Can we give them a spiritual bouquet of our family's prayers and Masses? Can we send them Father's Day cards, so they know our appreciation for their fatherly care? Can we send them family photos or invite them to dinner?

The sojourner, the fatherless, and the widow, third. Many Old Testament passages address the needs of the sojourner, the fatherless, and the widow in our midst. The people of Israel could harvest their fields, olive groves, and vineyards only once, rounding the corners. They were to leave the corners and any leftover produce for gleaning by those in need (see Deuteronomy 24:22b). We can adapt this practice by inviting people to harvest produce from our garden, vineyard, or orchard.

Everything we have is a gift from God; we give what we have been given. St. James reminds us, "Religion that is pure and undefiled before God and the Father is this: to visit orphans and widows in their affliction, and to keep oneself unstained from the world" (James 1:27).

Do you know orphans and widows? Perhaps you can include them in family meals or invite them for coffee and doughnuts, offering not only food but also quality conversation to meet the need for companionship.

The needs of the poor vary—from the essentials of food and shelter to personal needs. We gave cash to one widow (anonymously), so she could purchase her grandchildren

Christmas gifts. We gave another widow a season pass for soccer games, so she could watch her grandson play.

Our neighbor in need, fourth. Do we know the poor around us? "He who oppresses a poor man insults his Maker, but he who is kind to the needy honors him" (Proverbs 14:31). How can we find out who is in need and show them respect while offering them help? "Everyone must consider his every neighbor without exception as another self, taking into account first of all his life and the means necessary to living it with dignity, so as not to imitate the rich man who had no concern for the poor man Lazarus."[4]

Blessed Mother Teresa of Calcutta said, "Today it is very fashionable to talk about the poor. Unfortunately, it is not fashionable to talk with them."[5] Remember, like the Proverbs 31 woman, our care is to be personal as we open our hand to the poor.

HOW SHOULD WE GIVE?

St. Paul instructs the Corinthian Christians about their attitude when they give: "The point is this, he who sows sparingly will also reap sparingly, and he who sows bountifully will also reap bountifully. Each one must do as he has made up his mind, not reluctantly or under compulsion, for God loves a cheerful giver. And God is able to provide you with every blessing in abundance, so that you may always have enough of everything and may provide in abundance for every good work" (2 Corinthians 9:6–15).

The size of our gift matters less than the generosity of heart with which we give.

Give generously. God can work wonders through our limited efforts.

> Glorify the Lord generously,
>> and do not stint the first fruits of your hands.
> With every gift show a cheerful face,
>> and dedicate your tithe with gladness.
> Give to the Most High as he has given,
>> and as generously as your hand has found.
> For the Lord is the one who repays,
>> and he will repay you sevenfold. (Sirach 35:8–11)

Consider the little boy who gave his whole lunch to Jesus: five barley loaves and two fish. He did not count the crowd and decide his lunch could not feed them. He offered to the disciples what he had, and they gave the boy's meager meal to Jesus. Jesus then used it to feed five thousand men, plus women and children. The disciples even collected twelve baskets of leftovers (see Luke 9:12–17).

When we were in graduate school at Marquette University, several families—the Szews, the Klickas, and the Crnkoviches—invited us over for meals. The Crnkoviches often asked us to "help" them unclutter their fridge, freezer, or garden, sending us home with one or two bags of leftovers, frozen foods, or fresh produce. It was a subtle and gracious way of being generous.

Jim and Rachel, newly engaged friends, were grocery shopping on the way to our home. They asked if they could pick up something for us. I quickly assessed our needs and mentioned a couple of items. They arrived with several bags of groceries, including treats we never purchased. I fought back tears as they refused payment.

A couple of years later Jim and Rachel called with news: Their ten-month-old son was a big brother! Jim was beginning a business, and they were stretched financially. I could not afford what they had shared with us, but I purchased a large steak and two roses, one for each child, so they could celebrate.

As I entered their apartment, I spotted one lone hot dog floating in a pan—Jim's late-night dinner. I handed Rachel the package—such a small gift compared to theirs. She broke into tears. "You don't know what this means to us. We haven't had steak in so long!"

I assured Rachel I *knew* what it meant, reminding her of their generosity to us. What a joy to bless others with whatever means God gives us!

Give liberally. Consider the poor widow whose total offering at the temple during the feast was only two mites (see Luke 21:1–4), the equivalent of one cent. In the midst of plenty, this woman had needs, but she gave all that she had to the Lord. Was this an inconsequential gift? Not to Jesus!

Many gave larger amounts at the temple. Had they been stingy? Not necessarily. However, Jesus' point was that the rich gave out of their excess, but the widow gave out of her poverty. This poor widow is better known today than the wealthy who gave more lavishly. Jesus' point is that it is not about the amount nearly as much as the heart.

Do we give liberally or sparingly? As unto the Lord or to be seen by men?

Give sacrificially. The Christians in Corinth struggled with poverty, yet they offered donations for St. Paul's ministry. "For in a severe test of affliction, their abundance of joy and their extreme poverty have overflowed in a wealth of liberality on their part. For they gave according to their means, as I can testify, and beyond their means, of their own free will, begging us earnestly for the favor of taking part in the relief of the saints—and this, not as we expected, but first they gave themselves to the Lord and to us by the will of God" (2 Corinthians 8:2–5). Being rich in grace, the Corinthians gave lavishly.

Give freely. The book of Acts records the growth of the early Church. In Jerusalem many converts were added daily. "And they held steadfastly to the apostles' teaching and fellowship, to the breaking of the bread and to the prayers" (Acts 2:42). They witnessed many signs and wonders (v. 43) and shared with each other generously (vv. 45–46). Some even sold their possessions and shared the proceeds.

When Ananias and his wife, Sapphira, sold their land, they connived to deceive the apostles. They gave part of the proceeds *as if* it was everything (see Acts 5:1–2). Did they have to give it all? No! But when they lied to St. Peter, saying they were giving all, they lied to the Holy Spirit. Each in turn was struck dead.

We give without compulsion. There is nothing wrong with private property, so long as we remember that everything we have is a gift from the Lord. We make it available to him. When our children were small, we would explain to them, "Jesus gives to us *so that* we can share with others."

Give cheerfully. We should have no sense of regret or of merely fulfilling a duty when we give. This is joy! And our giving blesses our children as well. As the psalmist testifies, "I have been young, and now am old; yet I have not seen the righteous forsaken or his children begging bread. He is ever giving liberally and lending, and his children become a blessing" (Psalm 37:25–26).

In early marriage, during the years of graduate study, we were aware of needs around us but were unable to do much to help. Sensitive to that, we have begun a new tradition: We share some of our tithe with our children at Thanksgiving, so they have the joy of blessing others at Christmastime.

One year it included help for a crisis pregnancy center in South Bend; bags of food and a book for homeless people in Denver; a complete Christmas (dinner and gifts) for a parish family; a donation to the Franciscan Sisters in Toronto, Ohio, who run a mission for the poor; a gift of chickens, pigs, and a cow through World Vision for families in a developing country; and toys for local children. This is a tradition we hope will continue for many years.

Our children's creativity in noticing and then meeting needs around them blesses us all and inspires other ideas. What about offering scholarships for retreats, conferences, or schools? What about helping a seminarian with books or inspirational CDs or helping him pay off debt so he can be ordained?[6] What about donating books and inspirational materials to assist a military chaplain in his critical work?

By God's grace we can bless others as we open our hands to the poor.

CHAPTER TWO

Works of Mercy

Faith works, simply put. It is not enough to say we believe. If we believe, we will act like our heavenly Father, caring for those in need.

> Stretch forth your hand to the poor,
>   so that your blessing may be complete.
> Give graciously to all the living,
>   and withhold not kindness from the dead.
> Do not fail those who weep,
>   but mourn with those who mourn.
> Do not shrink from visiting a sick man,
>   because for such deeds you will be loved.
> In all you do, remember the end of your life,
>   and then you will never sin. (Sirach 7:32–36)

When we care for those around us, we live in the light of eternity. Jesus illustrated this with a prophecy regarding the final judgment:

> Then the King will say to those at his right hand, "Come, O blessed of my Father, inherit the kingdom prepared for you from the foundation of the world; for I was hungry and you gave me food, I was thirsty and you gave me drink, I was a stranger and you welcomed me, I was naked and you clothed me, I was sick and you visited me, I was in prison and you came to me…. Truly, I say to you, as

you did it to one of the least of these my brethren, you did
it to me." (Matthew 25:34–36, 40)

All call the King "Lord," but those who cared for the least of
the brethren inherit eternal life; those who did not are sent
into eternal punishment. Do we understand the importance
of the works of mercy?

FEED THE HUNGRY

Offer hospitality. Hospitality is not the same as entertaining.
Entertaining can be fun but overwhelming: the house
immaculate, the children nicely dressed, the meal gourmet.
Many young moms might feel as if they cannot entertain;
however, they might still have many opportunities to show
hospitality.

Hospitality is welcoming someone, communicating, "My
home is your home." This is something greatly honored
throughout Scripture. Not only is it a good idea to be hos-
pitable; it is a command. "Contribute to the needs of the
saints, practice hospitality" (Romans 12:13).

Through the years my mother has been a model of hospitality. Nearly every Sunday one or more of us, including Dad,
would ask if we could invite someone to dinner. How did
Mom accommodate all of our last-minute guests? There was
always enough roast, potatoes, and carrots for all. Those
Sunday meals fostered friendships, welcomed strangers, min-
istered to others, and modeled family life for us all.

"The presence of Christian friends or even strangers…
should brighten the home and enlarge its outlook, as the
guests tell of how the Lord has led them through the trials of

life and of the work that they are doing for Him. It is a good thing for a family to be jolted out of its routine, and to look out beyond the four walls of its own home and the weekly routine of its own business, school, and church."[1]

Whom should you invite? Jesus said, "But when you give a feast, invite the poor, the maimed, the lame, the blind, and you will be blessed, because they cannot repay you. You will be repaid at the resurrection of the just" (Luke 14:13–14). This means that you not only invite friends but also people who cannot reciprocate, such as large families, young families, or even strangers.

Large families. Someone cautioned me when we had our third baby, "Just watch: No one's going to invite you over for dinner." (Only large families and older couples who had raised large families did.) Two years later a couple with one child invited Scott and me over, without the children. When we arrived the wife said, "I would have invited your children, but I had no idea how much they eat." At the time my children were six, four, and one! Had she called me, I would have told her that altogether they consumed about one adult portion. We could have been spared the expense of a sitter. Later we moved to Steubenville, Ohio, and experienced generous hospitality toward our growing family.

Sometimes people hesitate to invite families because of their poorly managed children. We need to train our children to be well mannered and not finicky eaters, so that hospitality is easier for others.

Young families. Perhaps you could invite a family with a new baby to join you for dinner instead of taking them dinner. The recuperating mother might enjoy a brief venture out of the house, a good meal, some companionship, and a clean kitchen when she returns home.

Can you invite young mothers for soup and salad, giving them a midday breather and a listening ear? Or can you invite one young mother and hold her little one while she sips coffee and shares a pastry? These small gestures mean a lot.

Strangers. Are there elderly people separated from their children or newly bereft widows or widowers in your parish? Are there college students or other singles away from their families? "Do not neglect to show hospitality to strangers, for thereby some have entertained angels unawares" (Hebrews 13:2).

What should you serve? Do not get hung up on the menu! You can invite a family for a televised sports event and pizza. (We always have a Super Bowl party, no matter who is playing. We include singles, couples, families, and teens from the youth group.) You can set up cold cuts for make-your-own subs or just have a dessert of make-your-own sundaes.

You can invite families over for a brunch, a cookout, or a potluck after Sunday Mass. Or if you invite people over after a church function where you shared a meal, you only need to serve beverages. "Practice hospitality ungrudgingly to one another" (1 Peter 4:9).

Your guests can elevate the conversation. "Let your conversation be with men of understanding, and let all your discussion be about the law of the Most High. Let righteous men be your dinner companions, and let your glorying be in the fear of the Lord" (Sirach 9:15–16). As adults you set the tone of the table conversation; your children listen and participate.

Invite your parish priest, itinerant priests, or missionaries over, so your family can develop friendships with them. Can you include others in your holiday celebrations? Some people have no one with whom they can celebrate: college students who cannot travel home, neighbors whose children live far away, and single people who would not feast by themselves.

Feed others outside your home. You can contribute to food pantries, stretching your dollars by checking out sales on items they routinely stock. For special holidays you can fill and deliver food baskets through local charities, such as Meals on Wheels for shut-ins and the Boy Scouts' "Scouting for Food."

A Cincinnati mother, with her son in prison, faced a lonely Thanksgiving. She thought of others in need and approached her church with her desire to cook and serve a Thanksgiving meal for the needy in the church hall. Since that time, thousands have been blessed through her efforts.

You can take a cooked meal or dessert to someone who just had a baby or has experienced a family crisis. If you use plastic ware, there will be no dishes to return. When my firstborn was three months old, a parishioner left on our doorstep a marvelous roast with lots of potatoes and carrots (several meals' worth), already cooked. I burst into tears at her generosity. When our daughter-in-law Ana was ill with nausea during her first pregnancy, a neighbor brought a meal *every* Tuesday until Ana felt good enough to cook. What an amazing gift!

You can offer cash to someone with a hospitalized loved one so they can purchase cafeteria food more easily. Or you can take someone who is unemployed or recently divorced to the store and purchase groceries for him or her. You can bring your extra garden produce to church for anyone to take. Or you can purchase a meal plan for a college student who cannot afford one.

Our son Gabriel and his wife, Sarah, filled Ziploc bags for the homeless: a can of soup (with an easy-to-open tab) and a plastic spoon, prepackaged peanut butter crackers, cookies, a bottle of water, a napkin, and some inspirational literature. While we were driving around during my visit, Gabriel handed me a bag and told me to give it to one of the homeless men at an intersection. I did so—quickly! When the light turned green, I noticed that the man was already sharing the gift with another.

GIVE A DRINK TO THE THIRSTY

We can offer a drink to workers—a pitcher of iced tea or a frozen bottle of water that will melt in the hot sun. We can serve drinks in a soup kitchen. Or we can contribute to missionaries who are digging wells, so that whole villages can have access to drinkable water.

Whenever we have overnight guests (family or friends), I explain our open-fridge policy. I love serving meals, but I also want guests who are hungry or thirsty to know where they can find food and drink. I place a fruit basket and drinks on the counter, and I explain how to navigate cupboards for cereals or sandwiches.

CLOTHE THE NAKED

We can give baby showers to help meet the needs of young couples who are counting their pennies. We can purchase maternity or baby clothes for friends or for the local crisis pregnancy center. We can lend or donate gently used maternity or baby clothes.

We can sew clothing or knit scarves or mittens for the needy. One group of women who love to knit has formed a ministry of donating prayer shawls, lap robes, and baby blankets to hospitals, nursing homes, and crisis pregnancy centers. They also send their items to individuals for whom they are praying.

SHELTER THE HOMELESS

Foster care and adoption. Some families offer homes to children through foster care or adoption. They continue a tradition that began with the early Christians, who gathered abandoned babies and gave them homes.

Blessed Pope John Paul II wrote, "When he has no family, the person coming into the world develops an anguished sense of pain and loss, one which will subsequently burden his whole life. The Church draws near with loving concern,...[knowing] *that a person goes forth from the family in order to realize in a new family unit his particular vocation in life.*"[2]

No child should be alone. Could God be calling you to adopt or help someone afford an adoption?

Temporary housing. Some families offer a home to an unwed mother during her pregnancy. Others provide one person of a cohabiting couple a room free of charge, so the couple can prepare properly for a God-honoring marriage.

We have offered retreats for teens, college students, and women in our home. We have housed visiting professors and doctoral students and their families for brief stays. This has helped us grow in friendship, while saving our guests hotel and restaurant expenses, encouraging them in their studies, and helping everyone have fun. Opportunities are endless if we make ourselves (and our homes) available to the Lord.

Radical hospitality. Since 1990 our family has been blessed to live in extended household with thirty-five college students (one or two at a time, of course). Some have stayed for months; others, for years. Each has shared gifts and talents; each has challenged us to live our faith more deeply, allowing us to challenge him or her to do likewise.[3]

We did not invite high-needs people into our home. Other families might be called to that; we were not. We had young, vulnerable children whom we did not want exposed to unstable people.

We also waited until we were married for ten years before we began having an extended household. That way we could establish our family without close scrutiny.

We highly recommend this form of hospitality, with a caution: Know someone well before you invite him or her to live with your family. "Do not bring every man into your home, for many are the wiles of the crafty" (Sirach 11:29).

I count it a privilege to have shared life with many men and women of faith. Together we attended Mass, prayed the rosary, shared family devotions, prayed the Stations of the Cross in our orchard, and stood on the Life Chain. We enjoyed dinners and special Sunday lunches. We painted and wallpapered bedrooms, stained cabin doors, planted gardens and fruit trees, cooked, cleaned, and participated in various apostolates together. We also played games, watched movies, tossed footballs and Frisbees, shared music, and celebrated birthdays, holy days, anniversaries, political elections, and sporting events.

What an honor it has been to see so many young people move forward from our home into their vocations of priesthood, consecrated life, and marriage. At least four former household members now have more children than we do! These men and women have been—and continue to be— role models for our children, reinforcing our faith and values. Their humor, talents, skills, wisdom, and many acts of kindness helped supplement our parenting.

Multigenerational family culture. We encourage grandparents, parents, siblings and their families, aunts, uncles, and cousins to consider our home their home. We offer them a stopover for meals, a layover en route to another place, or a place for an extended stay.

We have offered our home as a place for our parents to live, should they want. Though they still enjoy their own homes, they know the option is there.

In our current culture people recoil at the thought either of being cared for by family or of caring for elderly parents. Blessed Pope John Paul II observed, "The times in which we are living tend to restrict family units to two generations... not infrequently due to the belief that having several generations living together interferes with privacy and makes life too difficult. But is this not where the problem really lies? *Families today have too little 'human' life.* There is a shortage of people with whom to create and share the common good."[4]

As Christians we see the possibilities of sharing life as part of our witness to the culture of life. What a blessing if we have the opportunity to share life with our parents as they age. God will give all of us the grace we need to do this well.

Build a home for another family. Scott asked how I wanted to celebrate our twenty-fifth wedding anniversary. I told him I wanted something different, something memorable. "Can we take our family on a mission trip and build a home for another family? We could all contribute; the oldest kids would be a huge help."

Scott already knew someone who regularly made these kinds of trips to Tijuana, Mexico. Scott was willing to go, but what about our children, ages twenty-one to five? They, too, agreed and promptly set aside the week we requested. We paid for the materials and all of our travel expenses.

We left for California on May 16, 2005. The following day we crossed the border into Mexico and began the first step: painting the boards that would form the walls of the house. By day we worked in blistering sun; by night we slept on cots in one large room, with no fans or air conditioning. In two and a half days, our family, with the help of three friends, completed a two-room structure.

What a blessing it was to greet the family who would live there, hand them the key to their home, and pray together. Though the wife did not speak English, nor I Spanish, we both wept as we embraced, mother to mother. "The essentials for life are water and bread and clothing and a house to cover one's nakedness. Better is the life of a poor man under the shelter of his roof than sumptuous food in another man's house" (Sirach 29:21–22). Our family received much more than we gave!

Visit the Sick and Imprisoned

Visit those who are sick. Your visit to people who are in hospitals or homebound with an illness provides an unusual opportunity to serve persons intensely and directly. You lighten their load by being with them and meeting practical needs. Pray to see the person of Jesus in the other person, as Blessed Mother Teresa did. If you are a eucharistic minister, you can bring Jesus to those who are unable to attend Mass.

When I took my three little ones to visit retired nuns in Joliet, Illinois, residents lingered in doorways to see or touch the children. One woman, upon one-year-old Hannah's insistence, spoke for the first time in five years. I read novels for a small group, wrote a letter for a resident, perused photo albums with another, played the piano, and led hymns.

Can you visit retired people in your community, especially with your children? Perhaps you can share a cup of coffee with someone who is homebound, or rake leaves, shovel walkways, or run errands for them. Or you could offer respite for those who care for severely handicapped or chronically ill family members.

Visit those who are in prison. Seven pro-lifers, arrested for dismantling an abortion machine, were imprisoned in Allentown, Pennsylvania, where we were scheduled to speak. The bishop helped us arrange a prison visit. We met first with the men and then with the women. Their cellmates were hardened criminals—murderers, rapists, and prostitutes. Still, the women had been able to save babies by sharing with pregnant inmates. We were privileged to assure them that they were not forgotten; we and many others were praying for them.

RANSOM THE CAPTIVE

Throughout the Middle Ages hundreds of thousands of Christians were captured and enslaved by enemies of the Church. Two orders were founded to redeem enslaved Christians through ransom or by giving themselves in exchange. In AD 1198 Sts. Felix of Valois and John of Matha founded the Trinitarians, and by 1787 they had redeemed 900,000 Christians. In 1218 Sts. Peter Nolasco and Raymond of Peñafort founded the Order of Our Lady of Ransom (the Mercedarians), and by 1632 they had redeemed 490,736 Christians. St. Vincent de Paul and his priests saved twelve hundred Christians in just twenty-two years during the 1600s, at a cost of 1.2 million pounds of silver.[5]

We need to understand who is being held captive and set these captives free. Even today some people have purchased freedom for Christians from their Muslim captors in Sudan. Around the world women and children are involved in the sex slave trade. Even in our own country, sex trafficking has ensnared many.

BURY THE DEAD

Blessed Mother Teresa of Calcutta touched the dying, physically and spiritually, caring for them as they passed away. She established a Home for the Dying and taught her sisters to care for the dying as if they were touching Jesus.

Out of abortion mill dumpsters, pro-lifers have collected babies' bodies and buried them on parish property or in cemeteries. At Franciscan University of Steubenville, we have a tomb where five aborted babies are buried; it is a place to pray and grieve. Typically after teen conferences, we find stuffed animals and flowers left there.

Some parishes have gardens where people can bury the remains of their miscarried babies in consecrated ground. Most hospitals make remains available or send them to a funeral home that provides grieving parents assistance free of charge.

It is good to attend funerals for loved ones, acquaintances, and parish members, as we are able. Our presence brings comfort to the bereaved and fulfills the Church's responsibility to accompany the deceased "at his journey's end, in order to surrender him into the Father's hands" (*CCC,*1683). Perhaps we can help pay burial expenses after an unexpected death.

Throughout the year, and especially during November, we pray for our beloved dead and for the dead whom nobody loves. "Give graciously to all the living, and withhold not kindness from the dead" (Sirach 7:33).

GRACIOUS GIVING AND RECEIVING

Jesus' example gives us eternal perspective. "For you know the grace of our Lord Jesus Christ, that though he was rich, yet for your sake he became poor, so that by his poverty you might become rich" (2 Corinthians 8:9). Jesus embraced poverty for our sake and taught his disciples to trust God for their needs.

For those who are poor: Receive help graciously. Do people know your needs? Do you allow people to show you charity?

While pregnant with my third child, I discovered that I had *placenta previa.* I bled off and on, sometimes heavily, and was constantly in danger of losing her. I needed meals prepared and care provided for my two little boys, ages two and four.

Scott's busy grad-student schedule was flexible, but I needed more help.

I apologized to a friend, "I'm so humiliated to call and say I'm bleeding again, but I really need help with these two little boys. I'm on mandatory bed rest so I won't lose this baby. Will you help me, *again*?"

She quickly asked, "Do you want me to go to heaven?" Her question caught me off guard. Of course I did.

"Kay, what do you mean?"

"If you don't call me and tell me when you have a need and give me a chance to help, you rob me of an opportunity to grow in grace, to grow in sanctity, to show my love for God. You must call me!"

She actually made it seem as if I was doing her a favor by asking for help! I thanked her profusely for making it so easy to ask. That was gracious giving, and I had to respond with gracious receiving.

For those who are rich: Give generously. This life provides many opportunities for you to detach from material goods by being generous. "As for the rich in this world, charge them not to be haughty, nor to set their hopes on uncertain riches but on God who richly furnishes us with everything to enjoy. They are to do good, to be rich in good deeds, liberal and generous, thus laying up for themselves a good foundation for the future, so that they may take hold of the life which is life indeed" (1 Timothy 6:17–19).

Whether we are poor, receiving graciously, or rich, giving generously, or somewhere in between, we honor the Lord with all he has placed in our care. We open our hands to the poor and share the joy of generous Christian giving.

PART TWO

She Looks Well to the Ways of Her Household

—Proverbs 31:27

CHAPTER THREE

The Parenting Adventure: Teens

On our first date Scott and I shared our concern about the dearth of godly men. In fact, we stopped mid-date to pray about it. Years later, after delivering our fourth son, I gazed into Joseph's eyes and prayed, "Lord, thank you for answering our prayer, though this surely is a *slow* way of raising godly men!"

The Proverbs 31 woman "looks well to the ways of her household" (Proverbs 31:27a). This means that she nurtures the lives of those in her household, no matter their age. For most of us this includes children.

OUR ATTITUDE TOWARD OUR TEENS

Each child is a gift from God. God is the source of all good gifts—including our teens. He has the wisdom and knowledge we need to parent our teens with grace, attentive to the child maturing before us. God teaches our children many things through us; and he teaches us through them.

Parenting teens—like parenting toddlers—must be done in God's strength, not our own. Otherwise we get caught in a will-versus-will power struggle in which everyone can lose. We do not have all the answers—I am not sure we even know all of the questions!—but God does.

Do we anticipate disaster or delight? How do we approach the teen years? Our attitude makes all the difference.

I visited a dear friend who had a newborn son. As we gazed together at this beautiful child, my friend burst into tears.

"What's wrong?" I asked.

"Only thirteen years till he's a teenager!"

I could not console her. She had lived a fairly wild life as a teen and obviously feared that her precious son would do the same. She anticipated disaster. I did not share her fears; I anticipated delight.

The teen years are the best, according to my mother. Teens think about the world and their place in it. They discuss life, love, politics, philosophy, and theology. They share their thoughts, if we listen. The teen years *are* wonderful years, though not without challenges.

There are similarities between teens and twos. This is not meant as a put-down of teens, but there are similarities. Sometimes teens amaze us with glimpses into their maturity as adults. Other times they astound us with temper tantrums reminiscent of earlier days—like two-year-olds with bigger bodies.

Teens and two-year-olds tend to be self-focused. They push for independence, not understanding that we are eager for their independence at the right time. Their bodies change dramatically. They can adjust to these changes, with our help.

All grown up...almost. During the teen years, children differentiate from their parents, seeking greater independence. That is not the same thing as distancing themselves from us emotionally.

We should not be fooled by an independent child who asserts his or her readiness. Maturity in some areas does not equal full maturity. Other people, not seeing weaknesses, might encourage our teen to attempt too much, which could set the stage for failure. We affirm what we can, guiding where needed.

When a teen hurries the process of maturity, we parents can caution, "You have to be your age now, or some day later you will be. If you try to act like an eighteen-year-old when you are only fourteen, someday you will have to work through the years of being a young teen. There is a time for everything. The advantages of being a little older will come in due time."

I had several debates with one teen about his age. He asserted he should be treated as a sixteen-year-old though, according to his birth certificate, he was only fifteen. His arguments included the following: "I am six-foot-three, and fifteen-year-olds are not that tall." "I am a junior in high school, and fifteen-year-olds are not that advanced." "I have responsibilities that fit a sixteen-year-old."

I rejoined, "The fact that we are discussing this demonstrates that you are fifteen!"

We love our children at every stage of life, including the teen years. We encourage them and believe the best. We focus on filling their emotional reservoirs, knowing that at times teachers, teammates, coaches, fellow students, and even friends and siblings will deplete their emotional reserves.

Though they are as large as adults in stature, they are still our children in need of affection and affirmation. Our ministry of presence may be even more important at this age than when they were younger. They need us to be available to talk after school, absorb negativity from the day, and discuss issues or relationships that are important to them.

Teens have a different interior clock than they had as children. Ever notice how the later the evening, the more teens tend to talk? Teens still need the discipline of bedtime balanced with opportunities for late-night conversations.

This is tough when parents are juggling a variety of ages. I had our last baby when our oldest was sixteen. I was up throughout the night with the baby, rose early with our little guys, and then talked with our teens at night. I prayed, "Lord, do you think I'm young enough to do this?" Apparently he did. Naps filled my gaps of sleep loss so I could parent a variety of ages at the same time.

Teens need us to be available. When they are sick, they need to know we will care for them without hovering over them. They count on us for rides to orthodontist appointments, sports practices, music lessons, youth groups, school activities, and their friends' homes. We may lament our "carpool drudgery." However, the time is brief, relatively speaking, when they will depend on us for rides to their events.

Celebrate the milestones. The McCalister family celebrates with the Birthday Box. Each child opens his or her own Birthday Box to discover a new freedom, one which that child greatly desires and is ready for. It may be the same freedom another child has received, but typically it is a freedom unique to that child. Parents anticipate requests and link freedoms with responsibilities. Of all the gifts they receive, the children most highly value their new freedoms. Here are some suggested freedoms to get you started:

Age seven: Have a friend sleep over.
Age eight: Begin a budget.

Age nine: Wear what you want to church.

Age ten: Ride your bike alone in the neighborhood.

Age eleven: Stay up until 9:00 PM.

Age twelve: Get your ears pierced (girls only), or drink coffee freely.

Age thirteen: Wear makeup (again, girls only), or visit grandparents alone.

Age fourteen: Decorate your room, have a cell phone, or bike to the mall alone. Get an e-mail address and be allowed to e-mail freely.

Age fifteen: Get a driver's permit and begin logging hours with Mom or Dad.

Age sixteen: Get a driver's license.

Age seventeen: Set your own bedtime.

Age eighteen: Have your own checking account.

(One choice that did not work well was the freedom to clean your room when you want.) If a child is irresponsible with a freedom, it can be lost until the next year.

In Judaism a boy has a bar mitzvah, during which he is declared "a son of the law." He is then treated as a man of the faith community. Today Jewish girls have a similar ceremony, called a bat mitzvah.

Scott and I made thirteen the age at which we celebrate our children's journey into adulthood. We gave each child a special ring and a surprise overnight adventure in Pittsburgh—Scott with each boy; I with Hannah. We enjoyed dinner, a movie, a swim, and lots of conversation about what maturity means. We arranged to have calls come in throughout the evening—from the men of the family for our sons and from the women for Hannah. Each caller shared a charge for purity and deeper faith. Some shared Scripture; others offered prayer or advice. This gave our children a sense of their extended family's support as they become adults.

In *Girls' Night Out: Having Fun with Your Daughter While Raising a Woman of God,* Michaelann Martin outlines a series of fun mother-daughter dates. She links the joy of becoming a woman with meaningful reflections on Scripture and a particular saint. The final date includes Dad at a nice restaurant, with a challenge for chastity.

NURTURE THE SOUL OF YOUR TEEN

Challenge your teen to choose Christ. Jesus set the example for his disciples: "Greater love has no man than this, that a man lay down his life for his friends. You are my friends if you do what I command you" (John 15:13–14). He wants his people to obey out of their love for him and not simply to avoid punishment.

Some teen ministry falls short because leaders offer teens something social rather than challenging them to live full-throttle for Jesus Christ. Why should teens try to live for something not worth dying for? If, however, they catch the vision for giving Christ everything, they will have a dynamism to their lives, especially if they share this vision with good friends.

Share the sacraments. As parents we never give our children a choice between poison and good food. Why give them a choice about whether or not to attend Mass on Sunday? This is nonnegotiable: It is mortal sin to miss Mass on Sunday intentionally. If they do not realize this is serious sin, we must tell them.

Daily Mass, on the other hand, is not required, though it is recommended. God wants more from us than fulfilling a Sunday obligation. He wants our Monday, Tuesday, and so on. He wants *all* our heart, *all* our mind, *all* our strength, and *all* our will. Likewise he desires this of our teens.

Even at the Hahn house, we occasionally hear, "Do I *have* to go to daily Mass?" My response, and they chime in at the end, is, "No—we *get* to."

Bringing my children to Jesus in the Mass is a great privilege, and I have a limited time during which I can exercise it. I want them to establish habits of godliness, which they need as they approach adulthood. Soon enough they will decide for themselves regarding frequent Communion.

Besides Mass, we should go to Confession and take our teens with us. We all benefit when any of us go. We want them to form this habit.

A good friend knew that on Saturdays her dad would gather the kids to take them with him to Confession. My friend said that routine kept them in check throughout the week. They acted differently on Friday nights than some friends, knowing that Saturday they would go to Confession. What a wonderful safeguard!

As parents we acknowledge that we all struggle with sin (à la Romans 7). The key is to continue the struggle against sin. Confession provides an opportunity for spiritual direction that goes deeper than absolution. "Indeed the regular Confession of our venial sins helps us form our conscience, fight against evil tendencies, let ourselves be healed by Christ and progress in the life of the Spirit" (*CCC,* 1458).

My husband has a policy: If you ask to go to Confession he will find a priest for you without asking questions. That is a thoughtful way to allow teens to deal with serious sin without adding the humiliation of telling parents.

Study the Word with your teen. We want our teens to connect the Word they hear at Mass with their lives. We give them a Bible and encourage them to read it. We memorize Scripture with our teens as a tool for guarding their hearts. "With my whole heart I seek you; let me not wander from your commandments! I have laid up your word in my heart, that I might not sin against you" (Psalm 119:10–11).

Often our teens need guidance, especially as they share their faith with friends. Scripture provides knowledge and wisdom, for "Your word is a lamp to my feet and a light to my path" (Psalm 119:105). This is as true for our teens as it is for us. More and more we glimpse each child as a mature brother or sister in Christ.

Do apologetics. Teens are going to argue, so get them to argue *for* the faith! Teach them how to defend it, "so that [they] may no longer be children, tossed back and forth and carried about with every wind of doctrine, by the cunning of men, by their craftiness in deceitful wiles" (Ephesians 4:14). There are those who want to throw our teen off balance or worse. Teens must understand why they believe what they believe and why it is worth believing. As St. Peter says, "Always be prepared to make a defense to any one who calls you to account for the hope that is in you, yet do it with gentleness and reverence" (1 Peter 3:15).

Encourage your teen to develop habits of holiness. Share spiritual habits you are developing. Purchase a journal in which your teen can record prayer concerns and reflections on Scripture. Challenge him to commit to a weekly holy hour—one hour of prayer before the Blessed Sacrament—especially once he has his own driver's license.

Ask if he is tithing. Once he makes big bucks flipping burgers, he might find it hard to part with the money unless he has the habit of tithing.

Invite your teen to maintain the discipline of regularly praying the rosary, the Stations of the Cross, and the Divine Mercy Chaplet. Find out when retreats are scheduled, and offer to pay. Share your spiritual reading, lending him a good book to get him started. Fr. Michael Scanlan's *Appointment with God* helps teens think about time management in regard to habits of holiness. C.S. Lewis's *Screwtape Letters* offers insights into the machinations of the Evil One to undermine a Christian's faith. Books by St. Josemaría Escrivá, like *Christ Is Passing By* and *The Forge,* are quick and thought-provoking reads. My husband's book *A Father Who Keeps His Promises* is a great overview of salvation history written at the high school level.

Nurture their vocation. One healthy way to help your child choose a vocation is to really love your spouse. Your generous, life-giving love prepares your child to be generous with God in the vocation he has for him.

Read lives of the saints as a family and point out that anyone can become a saint. Develop friendships with priests and nuns, so your children see they are normal people. Not everyone understands this. One little girl asked a nun, "What did your mother say when you were born, and the doctor said, 'You have a little nun'?"

Altar service gives children an opportunity to serve priests, which is particularly important for boys. Discernment retreats for potential seminarians and consecrated religious help them examine those vocations more closely. Never pressure your children toward consecrated life, but share the beauty of this particular call, letting them know they have your full support.

God has a wonderful plan for your life and for your children's lives. As parents you have your children's best interests at heart. Likewise your heavenly Father has all of your best interests at heart, including each child's vocation and his timing for revealing that plan. If you prepare them to be good spouses and parents, they will be prepared for any vocation.

RELATIONSHIPS WITH SIBLINGS: PREPARATION FOR A VOCATION

At one level a spouse is just another family relationship—shocking but true! The difference is that a spouse is the *only* family member a person can choose; parents, siblings, and children are God's choices. The harder one works at relationships with parents and siblings, the better prepared the person will be for marriage. Warning to young people: If you struggle with conflict resolution, communication skills, and acts of service with family members, you may find similar struggles with a spouse.

Great relationships take work; love is *not* all you need. The larger your family, the greater variety of personalities and temperaments you learn to appreciate and enjoy. How beautiful and complex family relationships can be!

Nurture deep attachments of the heart. "Parents are the ones who must create a family atmosphere animated by love and respect for God and men, in which the well-rounded personal and social education of children is fostered. Hence the family is the first school of the social virtues that every society needs."[1]

As parents we long for a communion of love within our family, though sibling interactions can resemble more of a battlefield than a love-in. If siblings' ages vary widely, they can be worlds apart in their experiences. How can parents facilitate deep attachments of the heart? How can we help our children effectively and respectfully communicate, value, and care for each other? How do we instill in them a desire to show each other respect and honor?

Regardless of the differences that separate our children, we pray that they will be close emotionally and spiritually. We also invest time and effort in fostering relationships between siblings that will last a lifetime.

Train children to speak the love languages to their siblings. How can they express love so that their siblings feel loved?[2]

Words of affirmation:
- On birthdays everyone shares a good thing about the person. Record the comments on a card as a keepsake.
- Cheer on and praise siblings at games, concerts, and other performances.
- Encourage children to write thoughtful thank-you notes after receiving gifts from one another.
- Ban negative humor: It hurts rather than helps.

Quality time:
- Work with a sibling on a project, like a pinewood derby car or a gift for a parent or sibling.
- Go camping or canoeing together.
- Take a younger sibling out for coffee or lunch. Parents can make a small investment in the ongoing relationship between kids by offering to pay.

Acts of service:
- Help children see the needs around them.
- If one child wrongs another, have that child apologize and do something helpful for the other.
- Remind each child of Proverbs 3:27: "Do not withhold good from those to whom it is due, when it is in your power to do it."
- Tie service to a liturgical observance: Be a Christkindl during Advent (offer a Mass or a rosary for another, or give another candy or other treats); mark good deeds during Advent by adding straw to Jesus' manger and during Lent by pulling thorns from a salt-dough crown of thorns.

Gift giving:
- Help children plan the money and time they will need to shop thoughtfully.
- Help them make gifts.
- Help them give each other lists of desired gifts.
- Encourage simple sharing: a piece of gum or candy, seconds at a meal, or a dessert they made.

Physical touch and closeness:
- Encourage hugs in greeting or after an apology, kissing a

little sibling's injury, and communicating tenderness and affection.

- Through sports: huddle to discuss a play, play tag in the pool, wrestle on the floor, give high-fives after a backyard soccer game.
- After the Sign of the Cross, hold hands for the meal blessing.
- Remind them they are not too big to show parents affection; it is why God gave them arms!
- A baby gives and receives much physical affection, which is great for teens.
- After morning prayer, huddle for a blessing and kisses from Mom or Dad.
- When a child moves away from home, pray for someone to touch or hug him.

Require teens to watch their words and their anger. When children are small, we teach them to talk; when children are big, we teach them to talk kindly. Sarcasm, flip statements, and cutting comments flow easily unless teens watch their words. Words are powerful, either to sow discord among siblings, which God hates (see Proverbs 6:19), or to strengthen relationships by resolving conflicts peaceably.

When teens complain about siblings, caution them to purify their motives: Do they want to see their siblings punished or helped? When teens are told something in confidence, advise them to differentiate between a safety issue—which parents must know—and tattling. "He who goes about as a talebearer reveals secrets, but he who is trustworthy in spirit keeps a thing hidden" (Proverbs 11:13).

Some conflicts arise when a verbal child and a not-so-verbal child argue. "When words are many, transgression is not lacking, but he who restrains his lips is prudent" (Proverbs 10:19). We want our children to desire harmony in our home, reminding them that "he who is slow to anger is better than the mighty, and he who rules his spirit than he who takes a city" (Proverbs 16:32).

Parents, know when to intervene. Sometimes the disparity between siblings is great in terms of maturity, ability to reason, and ability to argue. Their differences in size and strength can render them incapable of resolution before someone gets hurt.

Parents need wisdom to know when to intervene in children's conflicts. *Not intervening* can result in bitterness or resentment and painful memories. *Intervening too soon* can hinder growth in learning how to settle their differences. We want our children to develop interpersonal tools for conflict resolution so that they will be friends when they are adults. Trust them; they will understand eventually.

When Michael and Gabriel were young, they tussled with each other. Scott would challenge each one to pull one of his hands down to his side. With effort they would succeed. Next he would interlock his fingers and challenge them to pull his hands apart; they could not. Scott then would teach them, "Alone you can be defeated; together you remain strong."

The more our children show each other genuine love, affection, respect, and honor, the better prepared they will be for marriage. "Let love be genuine; hate what is evil, hold fast to what is good; love one another with brotherly affection; outdo one another in showing honor" (Romans 12:9–10).

Create a strong family culture. We cultivate strong family culture by sharing meals, observing holidays, celebrating sacraments, taking family trips, recounting family history, and establishing our own traditions. We ask our children, "How would you finish these phrases? When it comes to birthdays, we always...." Or, "At Christmas, we always.... " Their answers reveal that they have a good sense of our family's traditions.

We give our children a sense of belonging, helping them identify with our identity. They can distinguish our family's values. The stronger our family identity, the weaker the influence of peers to counter our family's values.

We play games together. We take turns choosing the game, so everyone gets to play his or her favorite every few weeks. Family game times can have an element of competition, provided competition is not the focus. When one son was devastated that he lost, I told him he needed to lose more. He was incredulous! How could a loving mother say that? "You need to lose more so losing does not sting so much."

In Stephen Covey's *7 Habits of Highly Effective Families,* he describes the process of writing a family mission statement. We wrote ours while on vacation. We listened to each family member, jotting down ideas without evaluating them. Then we wrote out the ideas with small corrections and called it our "Declaration of Interdependence." Everyone contributed, so the end product reflected the thoughts of the whole family.

Some families designed a weekend family retreat by adapting material from the Life in the Spirit Seminar. They mixed fun with sharing about the Lord for the broad range of their children's ages. The parents gave mini-talks; the children shared their insights. The parents then asked the older children, "What do you want to ask Jesus?" Praying over them was a very special experience.

The Apostolate for Family Consecration, located in Bloomington, Ohio, is a unique ministry to families.[3] Their weeklong Familyfests help families grow in their faith while having a lot of fun. Many families return each year, often with dear friends or extended family, developing life-changing friendships.

Discuss your family heritage. Talk with your family about the value of being a Christian family. Pray daily with your children for their vocations and, if it be marriage, their future spouses. Trust your teens to participate in family life, no matter how important friends seem to be.

God has entrusted these children to you—not to the state, not to the larger community, but to you. Just because society says your child is independent at a certain age does not make it so. "It is above all in raising children that the family fulfills its mission to proclaim the Gospel of Life. By word and example, in the daily round of relations and choices, and through concrete actions and signs, parents lead their children to authentic freedom."[4]

Let's continue building a strong family culture so our children can maintain their equilibrium during times of turbulence throughout the teen years.

CHAPTER FOUR

Nurture Your Teen Toward Maturity

As parents we nurture our teens toward overall maturity as well-adjusted adults, servant leaders, and companions with us on our journey of faith. We set short-term goals for long-term growth, so our teens are prepared for the future. It takes time to plant seeds, nurture growth, and weed out what is detrimental, so that at the right time, we can enjoy the fruits of our labor. We need wisdom, as do they. "Know that wisdom is [like honey] to your soul; if you find it, there will be a future, and your hope will not be cut off" (Proverbs 24:14).

In what areas do our teens need maturity?

Personal hygiene. This is an area of dramatic change from the child to the teen years.

After Gabriel's basketball practice, when he was just seven, I asked him to shower.

"Shower now? I showered after my game last night."

"Yes. Now you've had a practice, and you need another shower."

Incredulous, Gabriel asked, "Are you going to make me shower after *every* game and *every* practice?"

"Yes, I am."

"I just may quit basketball!"

I smiled, knowing this was a false threat.

Fast-forward several years. Gabriel showered regularly with no requests from me. Most teens do. They are aware of body odor. (If yours is not, politely mention that a spray of cologne will not do.)

Teens care about their appearance: their hair, complexion, and clothes. My children have uniformly chosen to do their own laundry, unsure I could be trusted not to shrink their jeans. My demotion (happily) means less laundry for me!

Privacy issues. Is there a secluded place for girls who are developing physically to dress without sisters watching? Does everyone get enough time in the bathroom? If children share a bedroom, can boundaries be drawn so the room remains orderly? Do siblings honor requests for not disturbing each other's music, clothes, shoes, or knickknacks?

Self-knowledge. Discuss with your teens the various types of personalities and temperaments. What impact does birth order have? What is your teen's role with older and younger siblings? What are his strengths and weaknesses, and how can you help him augment strengths and diminish weaknesses? Is she aware of physical changes, sugar highs and lows, hormone surges, and adrenaline rushes? Self-understanding is an important component of maturity.

Intellectual skills. Teens need good study skills for academic excellence. They hone skills in note-taking, researching, out-lining, and analyzing so they can organize and synthesize their papers and speeches. They grapple with major ideas in independent study. Amid major hormone shifts, they balance sports and activity schedules and develop a social life. Can they find a place to study away from distractions, especially the TV?

One parent insisted that his brilliant son run track so he might experience failure and develop character while living at home. We did not plan failures, but we did encourage sports, musical instruments, classes, and other activities that we knew would be difficult. Our children learned a lot; in some cases they surprised us with how well they did.

Sex education at home. This begins when children are small. But it is important to remember to listen before we answer. A child might approach his mom with the question, "Where did Johnny come from?" A detailed biological answer might be met with "I thought he was from Chicago!"

We sometimes assume children understand more than they do. Molly had a three-year-old, a two-year-old, and a baby when she discovered she was pregnant. She put the baby down for a nap and took the two older boys on a walk to share the good news.

"Guess what Mommy has in her tummy?" She smiled. "A baby!"

One child burst into tears. "I want to go home!"

"Honey, what's wrong?" Molly asked.

"You ate the baby!"

Quickly my friend assured her little son that the baby was quite safe at home in his crib, and the baby in her "tummy" was a new sibling.

We also need to give information on a need-to-know basis. My mother found herself in a dilemma when my three-year-old brother, sixteen years my junior, burst into the room asking, "Mom, what's in my pants?"

She thought, should I be the modern mother and give the anatomically correct name? Or should I do what I have done for years and be indirect? She decided it was time to use the technical term.

He broke into an infectious grin. "No, it isn't. It's a penny!" He reached into his shorts and pulled out a penny, at which point my modest mother wished she could retrieve her words!

When it comes to our teens, the focus of health education should be human development, not how to have sex. Most schools give too much information too soon. Mixed-sex classes give specifics on intercourse, contraception, and abortion. Yet they often lack essential information about the risks of premarital relations, especially venereal diseases, unwanted pregnancies, and possible sterility from abortion. Most of these classes do not address the beauty of chastity for the teens' well-being and their future families.

The goal of most sex education materials is clear: Break down a child's sense of modesty, and form a wedge between the child and his parents. The teen is encouraged to trust the Planned Parenthood lecturer more than his parents.

Can we provide something better? Absolutely! We honor our child's sense of modesty *and* genuine curiosity by private conversation about puberty and sex, dad to son and mom to daughter. We deepen our bond of mutual love and respect when we share the truth about love and life. Our openness allows for future conversation as needed.

For a son: Without giving details about sinful sexual behavior, tell him that sperm should only go where it can be fruitful: in his wife. Acknowledge God's gracious gift of fatherhood and his responsibility to embrace chastity so as to honor the woman he will marry.

For a daughter: Prepare her for God's design for puberty and the beauty of motherhood. Consider taking her to a

"Maiden by His Design" workshop for mothers and their daughters on these themes.[1] Explain the importance of modest dress and chaste actions, to honor the man she will marry.[2]

Encourage your daughter as she adjusts to her developing body and shifting hormones. Celebrate this change with a special dessert, discreetly acknowledging that she is now a woman. She may experience premenstrual syndrome (PMS). Help her accommodate that time of the month by lightening her schedule, getting more sleep, and avoiding foods that intensify difficulties. You can be understanding without indulging wrong behavior.

Financial skills. Your teen can develop a good work ethic. Whether your teen works for you or others, expect timeliness and follow-through. Encourage him to request clarification if instructions are unclear. He should not take personal calls or texts while working, and he must be honest about his hours and the work he has done. He could even explore career interests through apprenticeships.

We require work time as part of a teen's budget.[3] When a teen begins college, we create a budget for all expenses. We provide two-thirds of the budget; the teen provides one-third through earnings and gifts from grandparents.

Social skills. Teens' activities and conversations with the opposite sex can become interesting. They notice and enjoy the differences between them. Chapter five gives ideas for helping teens develop quality, healthy friendships without pressuring them prematurely into long-term romantic commitments.

Ask your teen what qualities—serious and fun—he would value in a spouse. This provides an objective standard for him before he invests in a romantic relationship. Encourage him to review and update the list periodically.

One friend saw his daughter's list and remarked, "No one but God could fill that list!" Shortly afterward she entered a convent.

One of our young sons said height was important. Then his older brother, Gabriel, brought home a gal for Sunday dinner. After taking her back to campus, Gabriel was eager to know our impressions. "What do you think?"

"She's only five-foot-two!" the younger brother quickly replied. "You'll ruin your gene pool!"

Gabriel shook his head and smiled. "You have no idea how irrelevant that is!"

The younger brother has since learned a lot. We *all* love Sarah—all five-foot-two of her—and are so glad that she is in our family.

My niece offered her list to her dad, who reviewed it quietly. He noted that he would not qualify, since one of her criteria was that her spouse come from an intact family. (His parents had divorced.) When she wondered aloud if she should remove it, her father assured her that he understood why that was important to her. He told her that though he knew his parents' divorce was not his fault, it had caused difficulties. That interaction facilitated a helpful conversation about what makes for a good spouse.

My sophomore year at Grove City College, I wrote a song describing a list of qualities I wanted in my future spouse. After dates I would sing it as a reminder of my standard. The only men who heard it before I was engaged were my brothers and my dad. The night Scott asked me to marry him, I sang it for him in Harbison Chapel. Later I sang it at our wedding reception.

PARENTING ON THE JOURNEY INTO ADULTHOOD

Recognize your teen's growing independence. Scott and I emphasize that with greater freedom comes greater responsibility. We say, as does the master in the parable, "Well done, good and faithful servant; you have been faithful over a little, I will set you over much; enter into the joy of your master" (Matthew 25:21).

We highlight our teens' successes while acknowledging their challenges. We limit some struggles toward independence by offering new freedoms. We link rewards with responsibilities, privileges with productivity, and money with good management. We warn that freedoms can be lost.

If we parents work more on our relationship with our teen than we work *on* our teen, we balance loving them unconditionally with trying to fix them. Then we imitate God's way of parenting: He loves us as we are, but he loves us too much to leave us there. God's faithfulness to us as his children challenges us to parent our teens over the long haul. We recognize their growing independence *and* their need for our involvement.

Discipline demonstrates love. When we give choices more than make demands, we demonstrate the respect our teens crave. When we give instructions, we expect obedience. Teens still need kind but firm discipline. Should they grow discouraged in this process, we remind them that discipline is part of genuine parental love. "My son, do not despise the Lord's discipline or be weary of his reproof, for the Lord reproves him whom he loves, as a father the son in whom he delights" (Proverbs 3:11–12; see Hebrews 12:3–11).

When we are disappointed with our teens' actions, do we differentiate between immaturity and sin? They are not the same. Do we acknowledge the difference between a teen's lack of judgment and deliberate defiance?

If we have a strong-willed child, we thank God. That child could be a powerhouse, *if* he or she yields that strength of will to the Lord. "Keep strict watch over a headstrong daughter, lest, when she finds liberty, she use it to her hurt" (Sirach 26:10).

Be diligent. Do not indulge your teen, out of laziness or lack of love. "Discipline your son, and he will give you rest; he will give delight to your heart" (Proverbs 29:17). Sirach says, "Do you have children? Discipline them, and make them obedient from their youth. Do you have daughters? Be concerned for their chastity, and do not show yourself too indulgent with them" (Sirach 7:23–24).

We can pray that disobedient children be caught and brought to sorrow for their sins. "He who conceals his transgressions will not prosper, but he who confesses and forsakes them will obtain mercy" (Proverbs 28:13). In the psalms the wicked seem to prosper. God allows them in their hardness of heart to go their merry way, knowing the outcome will be their demise. In contrast, God's kindness brings us to repentance.

If our teen protests that he forgot a rule, we remind him of his duty to remember. We share the truth in love at the right time—not before bedtime or when we have to go somewhere. We watch our tone of voice: Are we communicating respect and love? And we work on the relationship in times that do not involve conflict, so we can be proactive rather than reactive parents.

If we parent a spread of ages, are we changing how we speak when we switch from correcting a two-year-old to correcting a teen? When a teen acts up, we ask ourselves, "What does he need?" When he is least lovable, he most needs help.

The same moral standard applies to all, parents and teens. Require teens to communicate with respect, asking that the conversation be tabled briefly if necessary.

When I confronted one of our teens for not being in bed on time, again, he answered with disrespect. I calmly let him know that I would not accept that kind of response.

"Just chalk it up to the fact that I'm a teen, and I go to high school!" he quipped.

He was visibly surprised when I calmly responded, "No, the same standard that applies to you also applies to me. We must communicate with love and respect. I didn't come up with this standard."

He quickly acknowledged the truthfulness of what I said and apologized.

Sometimes parents back teens into a corner with a barrage of words, not giving them time to think through their attitudes or actions. We should model self-control and perhaps reflect more before continuing the conversation. If we compel conversation until it causes the child to erupt or melt down, that is disrespectful. We do not have to have the last word, though our word is final.

The appeal process. Teens can help us in the decision-making process, especially when they know the appeal process.[4] A teen can humbly request, not demand, an appeal if he has new information. (Whining or challenging authority should not be considered.) We respond with an open mind, seriously considering the teen's request. What a wonderful concept that encourages respect between parents and teens.

Problems create opportunities for growth, if we listen carefully. Stumbling blocks become steppingstones, provided we have the humility to admit we are wrong and make amends, just as we require our teens to do.

Day of Jubilee. Every seven years Israel was commanded to forgive all debts. Every seventh seven, Israel celebrated the Jubilee for two years (years forty-nine and fifty). A Jubilee was a time when debts were forgiven and land reverted to its original owner. This protected families from older members who might give away the family farm, so to speak.

Scott applied the principle of cancelled debts to our teens. A Day of Jubilee meant a teen could confess sin without fear of punishment. Sometimes a teen initiated such a day; sometimes Scott initiated it, sensing a troubled conscience.

The first time Scott explained this idea to Michael and Gabriel, they were incredulous. Was it possible for them to clear their consciences without being punished for their offenses? It was worth testing. Each came separately to Scott and confessed something; they waited to see what would happen.

Scott assured them that they would not be punished. Since that time no teen has taken undue advantage of this offer. When a confession to Scott indicates that sacramental Confession is needed too, he helps the teen locate a priest.

We can use a Day of Jubilee to express mercy and to keep the relationship growing. Our desire for the emotional health and moral maturity of our teens includes discussing their flaws, faults, and sins with kindness.

We lead our teens more by influence as trusted parents than by demanding obedience, though obedience is still required. Sometimes we must punish for rule infractions; sometimes corrections are enough. If we lead with criticism, we can cause a broken spirit and a broken relationship (see Proverbs 18:14). If we communicate love and respect, our teens will talk, and our teens will listen.

Keep parenting! Mom and Dad are a team. Each has insights the other parent needs. Mom should not shield her husband from the responsibilities of parenting, nor should she shield her children from her husband. Dad must not abdicate or dictate. The foundation of trust in marriage includes trusting each other in parenting. Sometimes a parent who is present has a better pulse on the situation; other times that parent is too close.

We may be tempted to excuse poor behavior as typical teen stuff. But how much is "typical" *because* we excuse it? Remember, our teens still need us to be parents, not buddies. Deep friendship will come later, provided we parent well through the teen years.

Sometimes teens feel misunderstood—and sometimes we misunderstand them. That does not excuse disobedience. Jesus knew his parents did not understand him when they lost him for three days in Jerusalem, but he continued to obey them, humbly following them back to Nazareth to live with them (see Luke 2:50–52).

Honor all. Mutual honor is implied with the fourth commandment, "'Honor your father and mother' (this is the first commandment with a promise), 'that it may be well with you and that you may live long on the earth'" (Ephesians 6:2; see Exodus 20:12). Parents "are the ones who gave you life, who introduced you to human existence in a particular family line, nation and culture. After God, they are your first benefactors. While God alone is good, indeed the Good itself, parents participate in this supreme goodness in a unique way."[5]

There is no age limit for honoring our parents. We will always owe them a debt we cannot repay.

WORKS OF MERCY APPLIED TO TEENS

We minister first to needs at home. It is more difficult—and rewarding—to care for loved ones who, like us, have not yet attained sainthood! We may be inspired by saints who endured great trials for Christ—whippings, beatings, deprivation, and death—but these are not the sacrifices asked of most of us.

What are ours? Giving one more cup of water at night to a child we settled an hour earlier. Laundering a uniform for a preteen after we have finished washing clothes for the week. Going out on a cold night, when we are ready for bed, for something a teen needs for school or a scout outing. Making one more doctor's visit before leaving on vacation, wondering what new germs we are adding to the mix while there. Our sufferings are real, and they are valuable when we offer them in union with the cross.

Here are some ways we offer works of mercy (*CCC,* 2447) for our teens:

- When we provide nutritious and delicious meals around a table of love, we "feed the hungry" and "give a drink to the thirsty"
- When we welcome children home to a safe harbor from the storms of life, we "welcome the stranger"
- By caring for their needs for comfortable, modest, and attractive clothing, we "clothe the naked"
- By caring for them when they are ill and offering comfort, we "visit the sick"
- When their growing pains for independence challenge our sanity and sanctity and make them feel trapped in emotional pain, we "visit the imprisoned"

We also engage in spiritual works of mercy with our teens when we:

- admonish the sinner (and help them get to Confession)
- instruct the ignorant
- advise the doubtful
- console the sorrowful
- forgive
- bear wrongs patiently
- pray for the living and the dead

SETTING BOUNDARIES FOR TEENS

Use CLEAR boundaries. As with younger children, we need CLEAR boundaries for basic discipline. Our policies should reflect rules that are *Consistent,* with *Limits* that are reasonable. We need *Enforceable* consequences that are *Adjusted* for age. Finally, we link privileges to *Responsibilities*. Our mutual respect and growing confidence in our teens help them accept the times we say "No" or "Not yet."

Bedtimes and curfews. In our family we set bedtimes and curfews until a teen is a senior in high school. Then we test his maturity by allowing him to decide both. We want him to adjust to this freedom while we can guide him, before he is in college. He can lose this freedom should he misuse it. All of our children have appreciated this freedom and used it maturely, with few corrections.

Driving. Privilege comes with responsibility. How will the young driver assist the family? Who will pay for gas and car insurance? (If a teen is the principal driver of a car on which he only needs liability insurance, the price of insurance is greatly reduced.) Can the teen drive friends, and if so, how many and when? In our family teens may not talk or text on a cell phone while driving.

Family policies on media. Parents need a united front on family policies for teen use of the computer, TV, cell phone, and iPod. It is good for Mom and Dad to establish rules before their teens compare policies with their friends' family policies. What are your concerns? You can invite input from your children without making it a democratic process.

This is uncharted water for our generation, since most technology today was not available when we were young. There is nothing inherently evil about these technologies. We navigate between leniency (pressure from our culture) and being ultrastrict (pressure from friends). We want wisdom according to principles, applying God's Word to today.

Be diligent rather than fearful. What are the pitfalls and

benefits of the technologies, and what parental controls are available? "Cast all your anxieties on him, for he cares about you. Be sober, be watchful. Your adversary the devil prowls around like a roaring lion, seeking some one to devour" (1 Peter 5:7–8).

We cannot afford to be naïve. The average teen is exposed to fourteen thousand sexualized messages per year through wireless technology and mobile entertainment. Pornography is seductive, destructive, and highly addictive, and now it is available in every home via the Internet. In fact, more than a billion pages of Internet porn are available, and pornographers hunt children via computers.[6]

We can limit our teens' exposure to temptation. We can also help them develop an inner moral and spiritual compass so they can quickly reject temptations when they come. It is easier to avoid temptation than to resist it! If porn pops up, teens should shut down the computer and tell a parent, rather than try to get rid of it.

Television. Parents should monitor TV programming and set limits. How much can teens see on school nights? On weekends? We require an hour of reading for either an hour of TV viewing or computer use. Parental controls are available if you have cable or satellite TV. Helpful reviews of movies are available on Screen It.[7]

Computer. Place a child's computer in a high-traffic area, like a family room. Utilize blocks, filters, and monitors.[8] A teen can circumvent this protection, so vigilance is vital. Work on your relationship, so your teen will not want to break your confidence. Trust, but verify. Decide computer etiquette: When is it too late to e-mail or chat online?

Cell phones. These devices are ubiquitous. Who should pay for the phone? If it is for the parents' convenience and the teen's safety, parents pay. If it is for the teen's convenience, perhaps the teen pays. How will you handle text message charges? Do you provide Internet access for your teen from his cell? Who will replace the phone if it is damaged or lost?

Remind your teen that you are still responsible for his well-being. You need to know if someone misuses his phone by stalking, pulling a prank, bullying, using sexually explicit language, or sexting. Go over the Safe Use Agreement from Pure Hope and sign it with your teen.[9] Decide cell phone etiquette: When is it too late to call or text?

Music. Music can be a universal language shared by parents and teens or a source of contention and mistrust. Know your teen's choices in contemporary music, Christian and secular. Listen and offer critiques, reserving the right to disallow certain songs and artists. Pray for wisdom.

TEEN REBELLION

Teens rebel against relationship more than authority. Rebellion is not caused by hormones, immaturity, or a desire for independence. Rebellion is a person's heart in conflict with God and God-given authorities, such as parents. It is a refusal to obey. If your teen acts rebellious, work on transforming your relationship rather than abandoning your teen emotionally because of your discouragement. "Discipline your son while there is hope; do not set your heart on his destruction" (Proverbs 19:18).

Broken relationships in a family are painful. Pain distracts us and isolates us. Relational pain is as deep as physical pain. We experience a sense of loss—who our child could have been—when we deal with the consequences of his or her actions. Dreams are shattered, with no simple way to return to normal.

We feel disconnected from our teen when trust has been broken. One mother's agony of the unknown was expressed this way: "I feel like I'm in labor again." We bring these concerns to the Lord and ask him for wisdom to rebuild trust.

We approach the foot of the cross with our teen in our heart. We relinquish our deepest agony to Jesus. Then God can fulfill his purpose for our pain. He does not want to crush us but to make us like his Son, for our good *and* for the good of our son or daughter.

One mother wrote, "In the midst of the grief of a broken relationship, we have a choice: Will the sadness envelop the day and be the focus of thoughts and conversations? Or will we focus on the good we can do for others around us and consign the child to God? May God keep any root of bitterness from growing." That is a great way to pray.

Tough love is *persistent* love. In essence we communicate, "You may let go of me, but I will not let go of you. You may not want to be with me, but I will take you with me to prayer." A great model for this kind of persistent love is St. Monica. Though it took years, her prayers and persistence bore rich fruit in the conversion of her son St. Augustine.

In the midst of this sorrow, we must stay close to our spouse, affirming unity. "Be angry, but sin not; commune with your own hearts on your beds, and be silent" (Psalm

4:4). We help each other guard against sorrow becoming depression, and we resist the temptation to blame each other.

> For sorrow results in death,
>> and sorrow of heart saps one's strength.
> In calamity sorrow continues,
>> and the life of the poor man weighs down his heart.
> Do not give your heart to sorrow;
>> drive it away, remembering the end of life. (Sirach 38:18–20)

Go to Mary, Undoer of Knots.[10] Mary untied the knot that our first mother, Eve, made. Through Mary's fiat, her willingness to serve, she untangled the threads of misinterpretation and mistrust created by Eve's refusal to serve.

Mary joins us at the foot of her son's cross. There she surveyed her son's sufferings and *still* chose faith, love, and hope. In the shadow of the cross, we too can bear our sufferings, trusting God, especially with Mary at our side.

Can our pain enlarge our capacity to love? When we feel any kind of pain, we recoil. We withdraw so we are no longer vulnerable; this is only natural. But with relational pain from a child, the Lord wants us to follow the supernatural way of love and remain open and vulnerable. Our suffering can release great grace in our family if we allow it to enlarge our capacity for grace. How?

I prayed for a word picture to illustrate this idea. I considered a barrel, a wineskin, and a womb, but each had a limit to its capacity. Then I thought of a well: The deeper the well, the more water it can hold. Instead of allowing my suffering to leave me empty, I can allow the Spirit to deepen the well of my soul, so he can fill me with more grace.

Just like a well in ancient cultures, a deep soul filled with God's grace is essential for the life of my family. This became my prayer: Lord, please remove more muck from the bottom of the well of my soul today. Then I can be more of a reservoir of your life-giving water—your grace—for my family.

The Scriptures speak of people digging either wells for water *or* ditches for traps. When someone digs a pit for an enemy, the Scripture warns, *that* person is the one who will be hurt (see Proverbs 26:27a). The difference between digging a well and digging a ditch is the intention of the digger.

How do we guard our hearts from digging a pit rather than a well? No matter how much pain we feel, we must desire our child's good. He is not the enemy; evil is. We will never receive from our child more pain, suffering, or sin than *we* have inflicted on Jesus. Forgiveness flows from our heavenly Father's heart, through ours, to others.

When we are bowed down with sorrow, we stay in prayer until God raises us. We do not push away the pain, nor do we live in the depths of the grief of it. We acknowledge, "I don't see the way to get from where I am to *where I need to be*, but, Jesus, I trust in you!"

Sometimes we walk through the valley of death alongside our child in her pain; sometimes we walk through the pain she is causing us. The essential realization is that Jesus walks alongside us both, guiding us and carrying us.

Prepare to welcome back a wayward child with forgiveness. Conversion is Christ's work, but you and I must cooperate. In the parable of the Prodigal Son, the father lets his son leave, knowing he will fail and suffer. Is that love? Yes, because the father knows that the pain will lead his son to repentance (see Luke 15:11–32). Has your loving heavenly Father let you experience pain and suffering in order to draw you to him?

When our child's choices have broken our heart, how do we rebuild trust? We do not offer cheap grace, but we also do not want our child crushed. When there is true repentance, we are thankful. Just as there is joy in heaven with the return of one sinner, there should be joy in our home when we share what God has done. For "the steadfast love of the LORD never ceases, his mercies never come to an end; they are new every morning: great is your faithfulness" (Lamentations 3:22–23).

We pray for the grace to parent our teens faithfully, so they may become the men and women God desires them to be.

PART THREE

She...Does Not Eat the Bread

of Idleness

—Proverbs 31:27

CHAPTER FIVE

The Virtue of Friendship

"She looks well to the ways of her household and does not eat the bread of idleness" (Proverbs 31:27). Does that mean the godly woman works all of the time? No; it means she is not slothful. She is not a *passive* parent, even when her children are older. She knows that faithfulness in parenting children to adulthood requires diligence in many areas, including the friends that her children have.

Our goals for a strong, dynamic family and for close friends for our children are not mutually exclusive. We want deep friendship within our family and good friends for our teens who will enrich their relationships with siblings. True friends strengthen and challenge each other to explore their common faith and interests.

QUALITIES OF TRUE FRIENDS

We want our teens to choose those who share their heart's desires, goals, and purposes. Their closest companions will influence them, for good or for ill. The following verses are useful conversation starters with teens about qualities of true friends.

True friends influence us for good. "He who walks with wise men becomes wise, but the companion of fools will suffer harm" (Proverbs 13:20). We imitate those closest to us. "Make no friendship with a man given to anger, nor go with a wrathful man, lest you learn his ways and entangle yourself in a snare" (Proverbs 22:24–25).

St. Paul clarifies the difference between sharing the faith with non-Christians and closely associating with those who are immoral: "I wrote to you in my letter not to associate with immoral men; not at all meaning the immoral of this world, or the greedy and robbers, or idolaters, since then you would need to go out of the world. But rather I wrote to you not to associate with any one who bears the name of brother if he is guilty of immorality or greed, or is an idolater, reviler, drunkard, or robber—not even to eat with such a one" (1 Corinthians 5:9–11). Jesus reached out to immoral people but did not have them as close companions apart from conversion.

True friends are consistent. "A friend loves at all times, and a brother is born for adversity" (Proverbs 17:17).

True friends are steadfast. "There are friends who pretend to be friends, but there is a friend who sticks closer than a brother" (Proverbs 18:24).

True friends forgive and reconcile. "He who forgives an offense seeks love, but he who repeats a matter alienates a friend" (Proverbs 17:9; see Luke 17:3–4). Friends should not let you down; but if they do, they apologize.

True friends tell you the truth, even if it hurts. "Faithful are the wounds of a friend; profuse are the kisses of an enemy" (Proverbs 27:6). True friends point out faults, flaws, and weaknesses so their friends can grow in grace and virtue.

True friends are empathetic. They multiply joys and share sorrows. "Rejoice with those who rejoice, weep with those who weep" (Romans 12:15). This is part of developing the art of good communication. Good friends listen well; they do not treat someone else's speaking as a pause between sharing their thoughts.

Do new technologies improve communication between friends or only increase access? Texting is not talking; chatting online is not the same as chatting in person. People miss important cues that come from gestures, tone of voice, and facial expressions.

True friends challenge us. "Iron sharpens iron, and one man sharpens another" (Proverbs 27:17). A good friend should change you, and vice versa.

True friends are gifts from God. Value good friends.

> A faithful friend is a sturdy shelter:
>> he that has found one has found a treasure.
> There is nothing so precious as a faithful friend,
>> and no scales can measure his excellence.
> A faithful friend is an elixir of life;
>> and those who fear the Lord will find him. (Sirach 6:14–16)

Have you noticed how often saints have had saints for companions? Some saints were relatives: Sts. Peter and Andrew were brothers; Sts. Monica and Augustine were mother and son; Sts. Clare and Agnes were sisters. Others were dear friends: the apostles; Sts. Paul, Timothy, and Barnabas; Sts. Clare and Francis; Sts. Teresa of Avila and John of the Cross, to name a few. They did not become saints automatically. They cared for and prayed for each other; they admonished and encouraged each other.

TEENS FOCUS ON FRIENDSHIP

High school years can be great years for developing friendships without the drama of dating. The mix of guys and gals can be dynamic. Watch a group of guys hanging out together, and feel the energy change when a gal walks into the room.

We want our teens to form good friendships with guys *and* gals. That is more possible, not less, when dating is not part of the mix. How can they develop friendships naturally?

Serve together. They can build meaningful relationships through service projects (for example, Scouts or 4-H) and apostolates. They can gather food for a food pantry or distribute gifts at Christmas. They can work together in youth ministry, such as Life Teen, the Edge, NET (National Evangelization Team), or Young Life. They can participate in apologetics groups or go on mission trips with a youth group.

Work together. They can work alongside each other: painting a house, cleaning up a yard, or collecting trash in a local park. They can assist elderly, homebound, or ill neighbors by shoveling their snow or raking their leaves. They can share common interests, working together on a school project, in a club, on a sports team, or in an ensemble doing a play or musical.

Play together. They can plan fun evenings for small or large groups of people, with some help from parents. Ideas include dinner for eight with a theme (costumes included), a movie night at someone's house, an opera or concert, brunch after Mass and then a hike, caroling and then hot chocolate and cookies, an ice cream social to which everyone brings a favorite topping, and an intramural sports event.

If your teens cannot yet drive, you can take a group bowling, swimming, ice- or roller-skating, or miniature golfing. You can transport them to sporting events, school shows, and movies. You can carpool for retreats and youth groups.

Encourage your teen to include others as they build a network of strong peers.

You may be among those parents who struggle to find like-minded families, even in your parish. Pray with your spouse, and look for ways to connect once you find even one other family. If you help jump-start a youth group for your teen's sake, it will be worth the effort, since the virtue of friendship provides strength in the spiritual life.

Pray together. The night before Advent begins, teens might enjoy a liturgical New Year's Eve party, replete with a countdown to midnight. Some area teens take turns in all-night adoration at a church. Others pray the rosary in front of abortion mills.

Serve each other. In imitation of Christ's example of friendship, St. Paul says, "through love be servants of one another" (Galatians 5:13b). Teens can help their friends study or do chores.

Include others. How do teens get to know someone who is not in their circle of friends? They can invite the new person to their lunch table. They can find common interests, so being together is natural. They can extend an invitation to a youth group or a dance.

Girls, enjoy the friendship; wait for a guy to lead. Do not give a guy anything you would not give a brother. If you confuse your friendship—using affection, little gifts, notes, and special attention—he may become uncomfortable with you, especially in front of others.

Give a guy the space he needs. When the time for deeper friendship is right, he will pursue you. If you let the guy lead, he will learn how. If you lead, either he will grow disinterested, or you will be stuck leading the relationship, which is not God's plan.

FOSTER YOUR TEEN'S FRIENDSHIPS

Establish clear family rules. We explain our family rules to our teen, making clear our expectations. Whether at our home or a friend's, we do not allow a mix of guys and gals without at least one parent present. We do not allow girls in our sons' bedrooms or guys in our daughter's. We expect their friends to be respectful of us, our other children, our rules, and our property.

Extend yourselves to serve your teen. We want our home to be a place where wholesome friendships thrive, where teens gather for youth group events, Bible studies, game or movie nights, or a dance. We stock up on food and drink to serve easily. We ask our teen to clean up, but we do not expect everything to look pristine. Our home is a place to use, not a museum to preserve.

When a teen requests something, instead of asking myself, "Why?" I try to ask myself, "Why not?" That takes effort when the request requires my service, since most days I already have a plan. When my teen has a scathingly brilliant idea—at least to him—can I accommodate him? It may inconvenience me, but thank God, my teen wants my help, needs a ride, or wants to host friends in our home.

Most teens want a deeper connection with their mothers and their fathers; we can offer that. We touch base with our teens as we drive or catch a meal out. We give them our undivided attention for a late night conversation. We work on our relationships with our teens when we can, treasuring the time, so that we have meaningful relationships in the future.

Finally, we pray for our children as they go through the teen years. They have many adjustments to make; so do we. We begin with the role of coach, but we move more and more to the sidelines. We trust the Lord to work through us as we guide them in a more excellent way of romance and get them ready for the love of their lives!

A MIXED MESSAGE

When strong friendships are forged, teens can encourage each other to be chaste. The *Catechism* says that "the virtue of chastity blossoms in *friendship*" (*CCC*, 2347).

In the summer of 1977, Scott did inner-city ministry in Pittsburgh with thirteen- and fourteen-year-old kids. He was to explain the Christian faith. He began by teaching a Christian approach to sex, stating that sex outside of marriage was wrong.

"I think you made a mistake," interrupted a teen. "You mean having babies when you're not married is wrong."

"Yes, having babies when you're not married is wrong; but so is sex outside of marriage."

"But sex is fun!" the teen interrupted again. "It's like playing basketball!" The roomful of teenagers broke into laughter and slight applause. They all agreed.

This was more than thirty years ago. What would they say today?

Have you looked at the materials that sex education classes offer teens? Some teach that there are four or five genders, not just two. Others do an exercise with a sack of flour, an egg, or, if the school has the funds, a baby doll with a computerized chip. The teen takes care of the sack, egg, or doll as if it was a baby.

The computerized doll records how it is treated. Is it held when it cries? Does it get a new diaper if it seems wet? Is it fed regularly? A magnetized armband records the teen's actions; the teacher grades the teen based on what is recorded. If the doll cries for two hours at night (which it is programmed to do), the teen has to care for the baby. He knows that shaking the baby will equal failing the class.

These can be helpful lessons, but what is the goal? The purpose is to show the teen what a burden a baby is, to discourage the teen from wanting "it." But this "it" is a person. Yes, a baby makes demands on Mom and Dad, but that is why babies should be conceived in committed marital relationships.

I once visited a friend whose teenage daughter had a computerized baby. The doll cried for two of our three hours together. At one point the daughter said, "I thought I wanted to have four children before I got this doll. Now I don't know if I want any!"

"If this were really your baby crying," I interjected, "your mother and I would be vying for who could hold her to calm her. She would look into your eyes, grip your fingers, coo when you snuggled her, and cradle in your arms for a feeding." I asked, "Can I hold the doll for you, to give you a break?"

"No, my wristband keeps track of whether or not *I'm* the one holding the baby." Then I watched in amazement as she stuck a diaper into the doll's mouth. Apparently the computer chip in the diaper triggered something inside; the doll quieted. (Hardly what a caring mother would do!)

What had this exercise taught? Not much!

THE VIRTUE OF CHASTITY

Chastity is an apprenticeship in self-mastery. It is a moral virtue, a grace, and a fruit of the Spirit (see *CCC,* 2345). Chastity is the successful integration of a person's sexuality in his or her state in life. "By divine vocation, some are called to live this purity in marriage. Others, foregoing all human love, are called to respond solely and passionately to God's love. Far from being slaves to sensuality, both the married and the unmarried are to be masters of their bodies and hearts in order to give themselves unstintingly to others."[1] We *all*, single or married, have to pursue purity.

We neither denigrate sex nor present babies as burdens to discourage teens from experimenting sexually. Instead we emphasize the beauty of chastity and God's plan for the joy of sex in marriage. The act of marriage *within* marriage is beautiful and life-giving—definitely worth the wait, and without bad memories or venereal diseases.

Flee fornication. Our teens should not confuse their social needs with sensual or sexual desires. "Shun immorality. Every other sin which a man commits is outside the body; but the immoral man sins against his own body" (1 Corinthians 6:18). Another translation reads, "Flee fornication" (*KJV*).

What does that mean, to "flee"? It means, run as if your life depended on it, like the von Trapps fleeing Austria at the end of *The Sound of Music.* If someone yelled, "Flee!" as they escaped a burning building, would we ask, "But how close can I get to the fire without being burned?" We would sprint. The question is not how close can we get to mortal sin without committing it, but how can we preserve purity?

Exercise self-control. Fire is an apt image for sex. In a fireplace, fire brings warmth, light, and a cozy ambiance. Out of the fireplace, fire causes destruction, damage, and death!

We want the home fires to burn but only in the fireplace. God has designed our bodies so that arousal leads to the marital embrace, like a fire. We want the fire in the hearth to blaze![2] We want a vital, beautiful sexual relationship with our spouse.

Self-control means that we control our bodies and our passions instead of being controlled by them. When we talk with our teens, we assure them that there is nothing wrong with a desire to love and to be loved, to give themselves completely to another person. That is a God-given desire, meant to be fulfilled within a committed relationship of marriage. "But immorality and all impurity or covetousness must not even be named among you, as is fitting among the saints" (Ephesians 5:3).

There should be no hint of impurity. Teens should avoid affection that can only be satisfied in the act of marriage; otherwise they risk defrauding each other, arousing passions they cannot fulfill. Solomon repeats the refrain, "Stir not up…love until it please" (Song of Solomon 2:7; 3:5). This is true even in engagement.

Sex is worth the wait. God's laws express his great love for us. They are intended for our good. After all, the joy of sexual intimacy was his idea. He established the boundary of marriage within which we can enjoy sex in a life-nurturing way.

While our teen may not know God's call yet, he can embrace what is clear about God's will. "For this is the will of

God, your sanctification: that you abstain from immorality; that each one of you know how to control his own body in holiness and honor, not in the passion of lust like heathens who do not know God" (1 Thessalonians 4:3–6).

PURSUE PURITY

Proverbs 31:12 says the woman of God "does [her spouse] good and not harm all the days of her life." *All* includes before marriage. Teens can make decisions for purity *now* that honor their future spouse.

Purity of heart. Purity of heart includes integrity in our love for God and for others (see *CCC,* 2521). "So shun youthful passions and aim at righteousness, faith, love, and peace, along with those who call upon the Lord from a pure heart" (2 Timothy 2:22). Self-mastery is one way we resist being a slave to our passions.

Purity of mind. Impure actions begin as impure thoughts. Jesus is to be the Lord of our imagination, so our thought life is pure. Temptations come; they are not sin. But what we do with those temptations can be sin. Do we reject or linger on those temptations?

Jesus warned that lust was not just a sin of action but also of thought (see Matthew 5:27–28). We are to "take every thought captive to obey Christ" (2 Corinthians 10:5). As St. Paul says, "Finally, brethren, whatever is true, whatever is honorable, whatever is just, whatever is pure, whatever is lovely, whatever is gracious, if there is any excellence, if there is anything worthy of praise, think about these things" (Philippians 4:8).

Our teens need to develop their consciences so they can resist temptations that will come. Sometimes, however, teens become scrupulous, overly sensitive to the possibility of committing mortal sin. A good priest can assist a teen in differentiating between temptations and sin. God's Word helps too. "How can a young man keep his way pure? By guarding it according to your Word" (Psalm 119:9). We remind them, "It's always easier to *avoid* temptation than to *resist* it."[3]

Purity of intention. By God's grace we develop mastery over our passions through greater discipline of our feelings and our imagination. We rectify our intentions as we develop moral virtue. St. Paul advised St. Timothy, his son in the faith, "Let no one despise your youth, but set the believers an example in speech and conduct, in love, in faith, in purity" (1 Timothy 4:12). Our teens can set that good example.

We need discretion in our conversation. "Like a gold ring in a swine's snout is a beautiful woman without discretion" (Proverbs 11:22).

God created men and women to be different in how we respond to each other. We should help our teens understand how the opposite sex responds: Women are sensitive to touch; men are sensitive to sight.

Purity of affection. Guys must be careful how they express affection, lest they communicate feelings they do not intend. How two friends embrace may make the difference in whether or not they protect each other's purity. There is "a time to embrace, and a time to refrain from embracing" (Ecclesiastes 3:5).

Purity of dress. Gals need to dress modestly; otherwise they can cause guys to struggle to maintain purity. "There's a big difference between dressing attractively and dressing to attract."[4] Dads can sensitize daughters by explaining how guys are sensitive to what they see.

It is important that guys and gals veil what should remain hidden. Tell your teens: Keep your clothes on; no nudity!

The power of purity. When we speak to our daughters, we might offer an analogy. Place a paper cup on the table alongside a beautiful piece of china. They both hold liquids, but how do they differ? The paper cup is cheap, easily damaged, and thrown away once used. The china is valuable and fragile—an heirloom with lasting beauty, to be treated gently.

If our teens value who they are, they will not allow others to misuse them in impurity. Our daughters will see themselves as beautiful vessels worthy of honor. Our sons will draw strength from the power of purity in their lives.

Young Catholic college men are banding together to "oppose a culture that accepts pornography, contraception and binge drinking." They offer each other a source of fellowship and support through prayer and practical ideas, so they can avoid the near occasion of sin. "In the University of Maryland group, for instance, each member of the group forgoes dinner every time any member of the group 'falls.'" And they define a fall "as viewing pornography, masturbating or engaging in sexual activity."[5]

"Two are better than one, because they have a good reward for their toil. For if they fall, one will lift up his fellow; but woe to him who is alone when he falls and has not another to lift him up" (Ecclesiastes 4:9–10). This is the virtue of friendship strengthening the virtue of chastity—the power of purity at work.

CHAPTER SIX

Preparing Your Teen for the Love of His Life

After choosing Christ, the second most life-changing decision our teen will make will be his vocation. It may be a call to single life that is temporary or permanent. If it is a call to consecrated life, will a son serve in a diocese or an order, and if an order, which one? Will a daughter join an order?

If it is a call to marriage, that will be confirmed by a specific individual to marry. Whom they marry will make a great difference in their lives.

Between the teen years and God's confirmation of a specific call, how can we best prepare our teen for the love of his life? The *Catechism* says it is "imperative to give suitable and timely instruction to young people, above all in the heart of their own families, about the dignity of married love...so that ...they will be able...to engage in honorable courtship and enter upon a marriage of their own" (*CCC,* 1632, quoting *Gaudium et Spes,* no. 49).

How do we lead our teens in "honorable courtship" that will result in a beautiful, God-honoring marriage? This is an area of wisdom, not law. (Please do not tell your teen that the Catholic Church does not want him to date, and that is why you do not allow dating in high school.) These reflections are part of what Scott and I have used in guiding our children.

First, with your spouse, identify the essential principles for preparing your children for lifelong love. Second, explore these ideas with your spouse, so you are united when you approach your preteen and teenage children. Third, apply these principles to your children with their input—every child and situation is different.

Whether you use the word *dating* or *courtship* is not as important as being clear about the principles you are establishing. Using the word *courtship* may help you define differences from the dating your teen is observing. Caution: Do not get stuck in semantics; catch the difference in principles. Courtship will look different to different people; wise dating and foolish courting are possible. The word itself is not as important as how teens conduct themselves in developing healthy romantic relationships.

Generally teens do not like being different. We can acknowledge that what we are asking of them is not easy, especially if they do not know others who are using a courtship model. We train them to question whether what "everyone" says is normal actually is; at the same time we are not being different just to be different.

Whether or not our teens feel comfortable not dating when they are young, they should follow our lead in what we believe is best for them. Their attraction to the opposite sex is God-given but needs guidance. "A bird flies not only through the force of his wings but also through the resistance of the wind."[1] We guide them so they can soar!

TYPICAL AMERICAN TEEN DATING: A CRITIQUE

Good news! You do not have to consign your teens to the American way of dating.

For thousands of years the family was the context for getting to know someone as a potential spouse. Since the advent of the automobile, the context for developing social relationships increasingly has switched from family to friends. Though teen dating is what most of us have known, it is a relatively recent phenomenon. Here is a critique of typical American dating.

Dating is just for fun; you do not have to marry the person! Dating is seen as a form of recreation, like volleyball and soccer. Sure, the opposite sex is interesting, and a mix of guys and gals makes a group fun. But once couples pair up into intense, one-on-one romantic relationships, the group dynamic is altered. In fact, dating in high school stifles social life. Couples' desires for more from a relationship than can happen at their ages produce frustration and temptation.

Some people find the love of their lives in high school, but that is the exception, not the rule. Maturity is necessary for a lasting marriage. Why allow teens to have serious romantic relationships when marriage is unlikely for years?

Age does not matter; some kids date as young as twelve or thirteen. Maturity *does* matter. Maturity is required for a couple to identify their standards and goals and to learn relational skills for a healthy, long-term relationship. In his book *I Kissed Dating Goodbye,* Josh Harris says dating when young is like window shopping without having the money anytime soon to satisfy that longing.[2]

What preteens or young teens experience is an entanglement of feelings and physical affection before they are capable to commit. They can learn lessons, but at what cost?

The more time a couple spends alone, the more vulnerable

they become to sexual temptation. They go too far too fast with too many opportunities, possibly even in their own homes, with parents absent. The younger the kids are when they begin dating, the more likely they are to have sex before marriage. In *Why Wait?* Josh McDowell offers the following statistics, based on twenty-four hundred teens surveyed:

Age of first dating:	Had sex before their high school graduation:
Sixteen	20 percent
Fifteen	40 percent
Fourteen	53 percent
Thirteen	56 percent
Twelve	91 percent[3]

Does this seem like an acceptable risk?

Dating helps you figure out what you want in a guy or gal. Teens want to learn what traits they desire in the opposite sex, but dating is not the only way for them to discover that. They learn what they like and do not like by looking at people they respect. Through relationships with their parents and siblings as well as friends, they discern traits that appeal to them and would complement them. They also see what they would *not* want in a future mate.

Trial and error in dating is like clothes shopping: A couple *try on* each other for size. Then one casts the other aside when that other is no longer interesting. That may work for clothes, but it does not work for people without harm to one or both involved.

Dating involves many relationships before you find "the one." Exactly! Serial dating (especially in junior high and high school) produces an emotional bond that is broken before a person forms another bond, which is broken, and so on. Bored with this one? Trade in for a new model. Someone new catch your eye? Move on to the next conquest. Through immaturity and sin, guys and gals cause emotional scarring that carries into future relationships and may establish patterns of fickleness and infidelity. This is more a pattern for divorce than preparation for indissoluble, lifelong marriage.

Dating often influences a teen's sense of self-worth. Teens are in love with love and with matchmaking. A peer group can influence one friend to pair up with another or break couples apart. Dating can add up to a lot of wasted energy. And one-on-one relationships often crowd out friends.

The danger is that teens allow others to define their sense of self-worth. Those who are dating may feel valued; those who are not may wonder what is wrong with them. A natural desire to please others can become an unnatural desire to become what others want you to be.

In dating, romance often precedes friendship. Friendliness is often confused with friendship. Romance can follow an attraction before a couple develops a friendship. This is out of order.

Friendship needs to come first. When a couple does not know each other well, they can pretend to be people they are not. Time spent with family or friends usually curbs this kind of gamesmanship.

Passion can consume time that a couple might have used to grow in friendship. A relationship based on feelings and sensual experience will be shallow. It then takes more work for the couple to develop depth to their relationship—not impossible but *definitely* challenging.

In dating, feelings can get ahead of clear thinking. Intimacy can confuse issues of the heart rather than clarify them. Hormones cruise through teens' bodies, combining with a natural desire to love and to be loved. Guys use words of love so that gals will be physically affectionate. Gals offer physical affection so they can feel loved.

Gals may not realize the additional challenge of desires being triggered by ovulation. By God's design, women are most prone to conceive a baby at the very time they long to be loved physically. Such feelings can even cause them to abandon their commitment to purity.

When these desires occur in marriage, they strengthen a couple's love. Outside of marriage a woman needs self-control and restraint. Being with friends can provide added protection for purity, as long as the couple refrains from inappropriate displays of affection in public, and the group encourages chaste behavior.

Dating can be isolating, limiting other friendships unnecessarily. A couple's goal may be privacy, but they easily can become isolated from family and friends. What sometimes begins as a special relationship within a group can become a closed circle.

Often a couple becomes caught in a cycle of "the relationship." They talk to each other about their relationship. They discuss their relationship with others, though typically without much parental input. It is as if the relationship takes on a life of its own—self-seeking and pleasure seeking—all the while each person desires something better without knowing how to make it better.

Good friends of the couple can feel excluded, especially those not also dating. After all, three is a crowd. Friendships often languish while a couple focuses on each other. When the couple break up, they may find their friends are uncomfortable and do not know how to include one or both of them again.

YOU CAN OFFER SOMETHING BETTER

If your children are young, share your thoughts about dating and courtship early. Explain how your family will function and why. Work with other parents to develop some adult-influenced peer pressure that will bolster the resolve of all your teens to follow this different but better way of thinking.

As parents we have to stay involved—no passive parenting! These are our precious sons and daughters. We have an obligation before the Lord to teach, train, and guide them, to prepare them for a love to last a lifetime!

It is never too late to make a difference in this area of a teen's life. Approach your teen in humility, and apologize for not talking more about this sooner.

When we asked one of our teens to take a step back with us, he responded, "I feel you are treating me like a little child!" His reaction was understandable.

I responded, "We're sorry. We should have talked about these things sooner, but we are also still learning how to be parents. If we were treating you like a little child, we would dictate certain things, and we are not. If you were in your twenties, we would treat you as an adult, but you are not. You are a teen—in between childhood and adulthood. We're going to give you input. We're going to have some restrictions your friends might not have. But please know our only motivation is our love for you and wanting the best for you."

His response amazed us. "This is hard, but I'm going to trust you. I know you love me more than anyone. Thanks for helping me."

If your teen is already in a relationship, it will be trickier to step back and establish some important boundaries, but do not be afraid to do it. Set an age before which dating cannot occur, or clarify that guy-gal social interaction will be limited to groups.

AN ALTERNATIVE: HONORABLE COURTSHIP

Build a castle. How do we prepare our teens for honorable courtship? Perhaps this word picture helps: Imagine a well-fortified castle in which you reign with your spouse as coregent. How can this be built so it is not just a sand castle? It needs a strong foundation.

The Lord is the rock, the foundation of a good marriage. Most of us do not think about that foundation, but it makes all the difference. Our relationship with the Lord takes a while to build and is mostly unseen, but it undergirds a good marriage.

Let the moat around the castle represent purity. It provides external protection for the castle, allowing it to be a place of family love.

The stone blocks that form the castle are the three kinds of love that Pope Benedict XVI discussed in his encyclical on love: *agape*, God's unconditional love, which is not based on feelings but on selfless commitment to the good of the other; *philia*, a kind of kindred spirit, brotherly affection among friends and family that leads to lifelong commitment and sacrificial service; and *eros*, loving physical or sexual passion, expressed at the right time between husband and wife.[4] These kinds of love build the castle walls; all are necessary.

Finally, the roof of the castle is the covering provided by the father's protection, the loving parents' wisdom, and the heritage of Christian faith. And the keep in the center of the castle is the soul of husband and wife.

Rebuild where necessary. The writer of Proverbs says, "I passed by the field of a sluggard, by the vineyard of a man without sense; and behold, it was all overgrown with thorns; the ground was covered with nettles, and its stone wall was broken down" (Proverbs 24:30–31).

Thorns and broken walls symbolize a life of sloth. We hope we have not been slothful in our parenting, but we all become distracted. We all have times when we thought we communicated to our teens something we did not. We may feel as if their castle is in shambles, covered with brambles. What do we do?

By the grace of God, we uproot weeds and repair walls. We restore what has been lost and humbly begin again. The Lord is continually rebuilding us; he can rebuild our teen! If we or our children have broken trust, it can be restored. "And your ancient ruins shall be rebuilt; you shall raise up the foundation of many generations; you shall be called the repairer of the breach, the restorer of streets to dwell in" (Isaiah 58:12).

WHEN ARE THEY READY FOR COURTSHIP?
Marriage is prefamily; courting is premarriage. If someone is not ready for family life, he or she is not ready for marriage.

If someone is not ready for marriage, then he or she is not ready for an intense, one-on-one, intimate romantic relationship. Even a superficial glance at a wedding vow helps a couple know if they are ready for that kind of commitment.

Obviously, God does what God does. Sometimes teens fall in love with their future husband or wife. Our task is to guide with as much wisdom as we can.

Work backward: Theoretically, when is the age of maturity for marriage? (It may vary from person to person.) Should your child complete college before marrying? Then how much time would be a good length for an engagement? For courtship? These considerations can determine when courtship should begin.

A person could be the right person, but the timing might be wrong. Scott told me our junior year at Grove City College, "If I spend more time with you, I'm going to fall in love with you, and I do not have time this year." He was right. The next year everything fell into place beautifully.

WHAT IS COURTSHIP?

Courtship begins with a well-developed friendship. It is a process that moves a couple from friendship to intentional friendship that is open to a permanent commitment. It is a serious consideration of an individual as a potential life partner—a relationship with relatively low passion initially versus a passionate, nonserious pairing. It tends toward a permanent relationship without a guarantee that marriage will result.

At the intentional friendship stage, a couple explores their compatibility based on the strengths and weaknesses of their temperaments and personalities. They talk about their views on faith, finances, children, and men's and women's roles. And they pledge to remain chaste.

Honorable courtship does not exclude other friendships. It includes family and friends, so each person sees the other in a natural context. Courting is a family affair, reminding the couple that each will be marrying into the other's family. As my mom says, "You marry the whole family." Other family members will be affected by each new member as well.

We hope we have a family culture in which our children will want to include the persons they are courting. The whole family plays a role in the discernment process. If a couple is away from home, at college or in their careers, planned visits to each other's homes include the families in the discernment process.

Even if courting does not culminate in a wedding, as a process it still works. The couple have honored each other and respected each other's families. If he is not the one for her, she is not the one for him. In the process they have not defrauded each other's future mate. A couple can experience heartbreak but still move on without regret.

Talk about difficulties with dating. Dating can be a waste of time that could have been spent cultivating talents, working on education, and developing other friendships. It can result in broken hearts, damaged trust in the opposite sex, bad memories, and a waste of money and emotional energy. For some it also involves a loss of virginity and resultant scars. The cycle of pairing up, isolating, being physically involved, and then breaking up may repeat many times.

Acknowledge difficulties about courting. A commitment to courtship may mean sadness and loneliness for your teen while others are pairing up in high school. Though group activities allow for friendships, others' dating can affect the group. Some friends may make fun of your teen for being different. Plus your teen may be unsure there will be someone special at the right time.

Pray through the process. Pray for your children as they go through this process with you. Trust that the Lord is at work in you *and* your teen. He will continue to work through you as you guide your teen in a more excellent way of romance. Share these ideas with your spouse, and pray together for wisdom to parent your teen to maturity, helping him be ready for the love of his life when it is time!

PART FOUR

Her Children Rise Up and

Call Her Blessed

—Proverbs 31:28

CHAPTER SEVEN

Raising Godly Adults in an Ungodly World

How long will it be before your child notices the sacrifices you have made for him or her? Years! You will nurse, dress, diaper, tell bedtime stories, cook, launder, carpool—love in countless ways—before that child realizes the depth of unconditional love you have shown. Maturity deepens that understanding, especially as the child becomes a spouse and parent.

The godly woman described in Proverbs 31 is a mature mother of older children. "Her children rise up and call her blessed" (Proverbs 31:28a). They recognize what a great job she has done. For what do they bless her?

They bless their mother for raising godly children in an ungodly world. Proverbs was written during a different time in history and in a different land, yet we face similar challenges with marriage and family life.

During a much earlier period of history, Noah faced these challenges of an ungodly culture. "The LORD saw that the wickedness of man was great in the earth, and that every imagination of the thoughts of his heart was only evil continually…. Now the earth was corrupt in God's sight, and the earth was filled with violence" (Genesis 6:5, 11).

God was ready to destroy everything, but Noah found favor with God. He was a righteous man, blameless in his generation (see Genesis 6:8, 9). God had a plan to save him and his entire family: his wife, their three sons, and their sons' wives. God commanded him to build an ark. Then he would send a flood that would cleanse the earth; those who would die physically were already dead spiritually.

Noah explained God's plan to his family. Noah's wife believed God's word through her husband; she trusted his leadership. Together Noah and she had raised sons who were men of God. These men also believed God's word through their father and helped him build the ark. In this godless culture they chose wives who followed their lead, believing God's word through Noah. (Remember, there was no priest to ask if they were on the right path, and there was no Bible to consult.)

Building the ark was no simple task; it took years. There was no Lowe's or Home Depot for materials. Then they had to gather the animals and supplies. "By faith Noah, being warned by God concerning events as yet unseen, took heed and constructed an ark for the saving of his household; by this he condemned the world and became an heir of the righteousness which comes by faith" (Hebrews 11:7).

It is safe to assume that while Noah and his family worked, the people mocked them—one of Jesus' sufferings mentioned in all four Gospels (see Matthew 20:19; 27:29, 31, 41; Mark 10:34; 15:20, 31; Luke 18:32; 22:63; 23:11, 36; John 19:2–3). And like those who would mock Jesus, these mockers did not understand their peril and did not repent.

Once everything was ready, Noah and his extended household boarded the ark and waited seven days for the rain (see Genesis 7:10–24). As the rain fell, they could hear cries. People were dying, including the families of the daughters-in-law, but Noah and his extended family were saved on the ark.

Jesus warned, "For as in those days before the flood they were eating and drinking, marrying and giving in marriage, until the day when Noah entered the ark, and they did not know until the flood came and swept them all away, so will be the coming of the Son of man" (Matthew 24:38–39). People did not know they were spiritually dead; they acted as if there would be no judgment. The same is true today, and like Noah, we may also be mocked for trying to raise godly children in an ungodly world.

We need to follow Noah's example. Husbands need to lead their families; wives need to trust the Lord to work through their husbands' spiritual leadership. We parents need to call our children to holiness, including choosing Christian spouses. And our families need to remain in the ark of the Church (the barque of Peter), so we are preserved from the floodwaters of wickedness that surround us. Finally, we thank God for the salvation he has graciously provided, praying that others will open their hearts to the same grace.

They bless their mother for their good family name. She contributes to a legacy: "The memory of the righteous is a blessing, but the name of the wicked will rot" (Proverbs 10:7).

When a wife marries, she takes her husband's name as an expression of unity. She then contributes to the positive reputation of that name. The couple then gives *their* name to their children and expects them to also contribute to the honor of the family name. "A good name is to be chosen rather than great riches, and favor is better than silver or gold" (Proverbs 22:1).

They bless her for her obedience of faith. The command to worship God alone concludes with this consequence: "For I the LORD your God am a jealous God, visiting the iniquity of the fathers upon the children to the third and the fourth generation of those who hate me, but showing mercy to thousands of those who love me and keep my commandments" (Exodus 20:5–6). As parents, our obedience or disobedience has a generational impact.

Likewise our marriage is an ongoing source of strength for our children as they move from childhood to adulthood. Christian husbands and wives are "joint heirs of the grace of life" (1 Peter 3:7). How we conduct ourselves in the vocation of marriage authenticates what we believe, especially in our expanding family. Imagine the gratitude of our adult children as they enter this vocation and discover its richness but also its challenges. How grateful they will be for our faithfulness! (My parents have already celebrated their fifty-fourth anniversary as of this writing.)

They bless their mother for her prayers for them. We pray for our adult children to be close emotionally and spiritually even when they are not close geographically. Time and space are our boundaries, not God's. When older children live elsewhere, we can feel scattered. We gather them in our prayers, offering our Masses and rosaries for them and uniting small mortifications and fasting to our petitions.

When someone sighs, "*All* I can do is pray," we remind them, "That is a lot!" We can light a candle in our child's darkness. We can harness heaven on his behalf in intercessory prayer. We can ask our guardian angel to work with our child's guardian angel. We imitate Jesus by interceding for our children, just as he lives to intercede for us (see Hebrews 7:25).

We pray for safety from physical and spiritual harm for our children, just as Job did. He rose early daily to pray for his adult children, that they might not sin grievously against the Lord (see Job 1:5). His prayers formed a hedge of protection that only God could allow Satan to breach (Job 1:10). Like Job, we ask God to forgive our child for any venial sins, "and God will give him life for those whose sin is not deadly" (1 John 5:16).

We pray for a godly spouse from a godly family for each child called to marriage. It is not enough to raise a godly child; *whom* they marry is also critical. We also pray for the whole family into which our child will marry. One college student, dating a strong Catholic whose father now rejects the faith, said, "It's hard to face a dad who sees my being a strong Catholic man as a liability to overcome." That is sobering.

The people who formed our son's wife or our daughter's husband will be ongoing influences. We pray that they will strengthen the couple and support them as they parent. They will be the other grandparents of our grandchildren.

GUIDANCE FOR MARRIAGE

Desire a Christian marriage. Too few Catholics talk about their desire for their children to marry believers. It is not enough to find someone *willing* to let the grandchildren be raised Catholic. They need to share the faith. Marriage is tough enough when you are on the same page spiritually.

St. Paul has strong words about marrying unbelievers: "Do not be mismated with unbelievers. For what partnership have righteousness and iniquity? Or what fellowship has light with darkness? What accord has Christ with Belial? Or what has a believer in common with an unbeliever?" (2 Corinthians 6:14–15).

What if a young adult affirms the advice of not marrying an unbeliever but wants to date one? This person does not understand the ways of love and how easily principles can be compromised. She needs to distrust her own heart. It is possible to fall in love with someone whose religious views are radically different from one's own. There are moral non-Christians, but that does not make them suitable life partners.

What if a young adult wants to date a non-Christian so he can evangelize her? It sounds noble, but it is presumptuous to say, "I'll make her a Christian!" He should not confuse his role in her life with that of the Holy Spirit, even though it would be best for her to become a Christian. He is not respecting her free will if he pressures her to change. She needs to make that decision for Christ apart from whether or not she will keep or lose him as a boyfriend or spouse.

Better to share the faith with her as a friend, apart from a romantic relationship. Should she become a Christian, then dating would be possible.

If a young adult marries an unbaptized person, their marriage may be valid but not sacramental, because the baptized bride and groom are the very ministers of the sacrament. Jesus said, "Do you think that I have come to give peace on earth? No, I tell you, but rather division" (Luke 12:51). In a family where one is a believer and one is not, there can be terrible dissension.

Desire a Catholic marriage. Unity of rite is also important. Scott and I began marriage one in heart and mind as Presbyterians, and his conversion to Catholicism predated mine by four years. Since we lived in a mixed marriage for those years, some women have sought our approval of it, saying, "You made it work." What they do not understand is the agony that both Scott and I endured during those four years. I would not have dated a Catholic, but suddenly I was married to one—and no ordinary Catholic either![1]

We were again at peace with one another after I became Catholic. We are not guaranteed a perfect marriage just because we share the same rite; after all, we are imperfect people. But our united spiritual life is a firm foundation for marriage and family life.

Practical preparation. Besides the spiritual foundation, we also pray for our sons' preparation for providing for a wife and children.[2] As much as possible, a man should develop his career before he builds his family. "Prepare your work outside, get everything ready for you in the field; and after that build your house" (Proverbs 24:27). Here *house* means *family*, rather than the structure of a home. This is general wisdom. The application to specific children depends upon how God leads them.

Scott cautions gals at Franciscan University to be patient with the guys on campus. School is a time of preparation for a career, and guys can feel unsure how they will provide for a wife and family. Scott says, "As is true of many species, males don't mate well in captivity." So, gals, let the guys get their education under their belt, and then they will be ready for a serious relationship.

Daughters should prepare for their role as nurturers and homemakers. Like Rebekah, Rachel, and Abigail in the Old Testament, they need to "go to the well." In the midst of doing ordinary work, these three women were surprised by joy in discovering their true love. As daughters pursue their ordinary tasks, they also will discover God's call on their lives.

Finally, we talk with all of our children about establishing and following a budget, avoiding debt, managing credit cards, and above all, living within their means.[3] This is excellent preparation for marriage, since money issues are a primary source of marital conflict.

ADULT-TO-ADULT COMMUNICATION

We communicate love and respect. We model love and respect to our maturing children as added training for marriage. One of our principles for conflict resolution is keeping short accounts. We talk through minor conflicts so that they do not become major. We cannot demand this of our adult children, but it is our consistent family pattern. We leave space for grace to work and try to discuss difficulties openly.

We aim to forgive from the heart without strings attached, whether or not the other person asks for forgiveness. When we do not live in the same house and have unresolved conflicts, physical distance can become emotional distance. Noncommunication can be difficult to discern: Is it silent treatment or space for resolving differences, with fewer words that could increase conflict? We must not nurture feelings of being wronged, and we should not recount incidents to other children.

We never stop parenting, but we move into a new phase in which we offer advice mostly by invitation. We focus on support and encouragement. We make more emotional deposits and fewer withdrawals (criticisms), especially if our time together is limited.

We allow control of the relationship to shift. As our children move into adulthood, control shifts. We step back, allowing the young adult to set the pace.

My dear friend Amy, after adopting an older child, reflected on similarities between that and parenting young adults:

> We must have the courage and the patience to wait until they ask. At the same time there are occasions when we have to trust our intuition and push a bit harder because they can't ask or don't know how to ask for help they need.
>
> Adult children are not rejecting us; they are rejecting the level of parenting that has been the norm, in order to establish themselves as adults. We cannot let our need to be needed nor our need to be in control get in the way. There are new rules, and we are not the ones setting them. It helps if we voluntarily step back, giving them more space for independence.
>
> Some conflict will come from immaturity, but pressing that point will not improve it. Stepping back might diffuse tension, lessening pressure instead of adding to it. How can we make an adult child "be good"? We cannot, but we can pray that they will make good choices.

Our young adults need to know we trust *God* to be in control of the relationship. We can relinquish control without disconnecting from them. We ask them about their needs; if we can help, we will. If they do not want our help, we respect that. We let them know of our desire to be together but give them the freedom to choose.

They will see our flaws, weaknesses, and sins in sharper focus. They may recognize times they felt hurt when they were younger, whether or not we intended hurt. Instead of seeing these incidences as sad moments of reality, we recognize them as moments of grace and restoration. We thank God for the opportunity to ask for forgiveness, undoing damage now that that incident has surfaced. We model behavior for our young adult children that they will need when they are older. For just as surely, our children will someday need to apologize to their children for their shortcomings and sins.

We love from a distance. As mothers of young children, we seemed surrounded by our little ones; their lives revolved around us. As our children mature in the teen years and beyond, our lives revolve more around theirs. (A mix of ages in a family can be dizzying, as parents do both.) Whether our adult children are single or married, we want to give them the sense that we are undergirding them without crowding them.

We may welcome them back home for a time. Sometimes a young adult wants to move home. This can be a wonderful time for reestablishing close relationships, provided we clarify expectations and boundaries. Ground rules help lessen stress as we learn to live together again.

My sister Kari and her husband, Mark, established rules for their college-age children who live at home. Their goal was to clarify expectations, not to make the kids feel little again. In brief, here are their rules:

- Bedroom—daily: Make bed, pick up clothes, and put clean clothes away; weekly: Dust and sweep the room and collect trash.
- Bathroom—daily: Hang towels; weekly: Collect trash, clean sink, toilet, and shower or tub.
- Other floors—daily: Put belongings away; weekly: Help with cleaning chores.
- Common courtesies: Tell us if you will miss dinner, where you will be, and when you will be home. Be home by midnight. Talk to parents and siblings with respect. Any moving violations with a family car result in driver's payment of ticket *and* future car insurance.
- Penalties: Loss of cell phone use for a week, loss of car privileges for a week, or increase in tasks around the house.

Our culture says that an eighteen-year-old is emancipated. The *Catechism,* however, says, "As long as a child lives at home with his parents, the child should obey his parents in all that they ask of him when it is for his good or that of the family" (*CCC,* 2217).

Older siblings need to be aware of what their presence means to younger siblings. The younger watch and want to imitate the older. As older children return home, all may have more adjustments than they anticipated.

Some families ask the adult returning home for money toward food and utilities; some do not. Your child needs to contribute to life at home in some way. If your adult child can avoid or get out of debt, it would be better for him to live at home and help rather than spend more money. However, if you sense that your adult child is taking advantage of your generosity, you may need tough love that offers emotional support but no longer includes financial help. He may have to get his own apartment.

We had a beautiful experience when Hannah moved home during her last semester of college. Through conversations, enjoying a movie or a TV series, and sharing meals, she reestablished friendships with her brothers at home. For two years she contributed to our meals by cooking and entertaining us as the "Carb Comic," and she filled our home with her beautiful music. We are so grateful for that time.

Young adults must honor their parents. Young adults, single or married, are obligated to honor their parents. Honor is not the same as obedience. "As they grow up, children should continue to respect their parents. They should anticipate their wishes, willingly seek their advice, and accept their just admonitions. Obedience toward parents ceases with the emancipation of the children; not so respect, which is always owed to them. This respect has its roots in the fear of God, one of the gifts of the Holy Spirit" (*CCC*, 2217).

We owe our parents a debt of gratitude we can never repay for the gifts of life, love, and labor they have given—and continue to give (see Sirach 7:27–28; Proverbs 23:22). Our children owe the same debt to us.

ADVICE TO A YOUNG ADULT: LIVE YOUR SINGLENESS RICHLY

As our teens move toward adulthood, they long to share life with someone committed to them for life. They want to reveal themselves to another. They desire to share the reservoir of love and affection that till now they have held in reserve. How do we help them in the in-between time of singleness, especially when we do not know how long that will last?

Do not waste this time. We tell our young adults: Let God be your first and best love. Give him the depth of love you desire to share with another. You were created for intimate communion with the One who made and redeemed you, and there are some needs only he can fill.

In the grand scheme of things, this time may be brief; do not waste it. Trust God's timing, and try not to act as if life is on hold. Do not act as if you are treading water until life becomes meaningful because of a particular man or woman. Instead, value being single. *Live* your singleness richly and without regret to the glory of God. Develop your talents, skills, abilities, mind, and faith, so that you can respond to God's call when it becomes clear. This time is a gift to prepare you for that call.

Pray for your future spouse. Encourage your young adults: You can be part of your future spouse's life today through prayer. You can record reflections in a journal you will some-day share—for example, "I saw the same moon you saw tonight, and I prayed that God would give you a great day tomorrow."

Thank God always. Challenge your young adults: Thank God for your current circumstance. "Thank God that I am single?" Yes! "Rejoice always, pray constantly, give thanks in all circumstances; for this is the will of God in Christ Jesus for you" (1 Thessalonians 5:16–18).

"The joy of the LORD is your strength" (Nehemiah 8:10), so resist any temptation to sadness. Who is the source of your hope, your joy, your security? God alone.

Marriage is a particular call to a particular person. Remind your young adults: You are not looking for "*a* love life" but "*the* love of your life." You are not called to marriage in general but to someone in particular. God will reveal that call at the right time.

Consider Adam and Eve. God created Eve without Adam's active assistance. God did not set her loose in the garden to hunt for Adam, nor did he tell Adam to find Eve. At the right time, God presented Eve to Adam. And he will do the same for you.

God has a wonderful plan for your life! Meanwhile, let God recreate you so that you are ready for that relationship. "For I know the plans I have for you, says the LORD, plans for welfare and not for evil, to give you a future and a hope" (Jeremiah 29:11).

Choose your spouse wisely. Caution your young adults: Your vocation, whether it be consecrated single life, religious life, or marriage, is an essential part of your journey toward heaven. If your call is marriage, then your spouse will be your most important companion on your spiritual journey— someone who first has entrusted his heart to God and then is trustworthy with your heart. Pray for wisdom, and then apply wisdom to your choice for a spouse.

CHAPTER EIGHT

Honorable Courtship

Is courtship possible? Yes! Growing numbers of young couples are looking for something more than Christian rules for dating. They are choosing courtship. They are building on a solid friendship to see if it will mature naturally into a serious relationship.

Though guidance for courtship may vary from family to family, here are some thoughts to discuss with your children. There is a better way than typical American dating!

READY TO COURT?

Here are some questions for your son or daughter to consider before courting:

- Does this person inspire you to love the Lord and the Church more?
- Do you already have a good friendship?
- Do you desire to become like this person?
- What is the quality of his or her relationships with family? Friends?
- Does the time you spend together in friendship build your character?
- What differences do you have: Economic? Cultural? Age? Education? Political?
- How does this person handle anger and resolve conflicts?
- Does this person respond to authority with respect and humility or with dishonor and self-righteousness?

- Are you really attracted to this person? (There needs to be zing!)
- What are the loves of his or her life?

If the young man feels ready, the next step is for him to request permission to court.

ASK HER DAD

When I shared this idea with Michael, he was taken aback. Asking the father for a young lady's hand in marriage was something he had assumed, but asking if he could court seemed excessive, even embarrassing.

I asked God to give me a word picture that would help me explain the idea better, and my eyes lit on the neighbor's bright red sports car.

"Michael, do you see the neighbor's sports car?"

"Yeah."

"Would you like to drive that car?"

"Sure."

"What would you do if you wanted to take it for a spin? You would talk to the owner. You would mention that you are a good driver, that you are insured, and that your parents would vouch for you. Then you would ask permission to drive the car, not assuming that permission would be given, wouldn't you?"

"I see where this is going," Michael said, shaking his head.

I smiled. "Is the neighbor's daughter less valuable than his car?"

"That's not fair," Michael protested, breaking into a smile.

A young man will never go wrong acknowledging a father's

authority in his daughter's life. He is honored to be asked. Then the father can speak privately to his daughter to be sure of her desire. If a father is not in the picture, due to death or divorce, the young man should ask the mother. If the word *court* bothers a guy, he could ask permission to "date" the young woman.

What happens if a couple meets in college? If the young man lives far from the woman's family, the request may be made by phone. After our son Gabriel had built a solid friendship with Sarah, he called her father and asked if he could court her. Her father readily gave him permission.

HOW TO COURT

Deepen the friendship. The goal is to get to know each other much better, moving from friendship to intentional friendship that is exclusive. Different contexts help people see each other in a different light.

It is good for a couple to spend time together in situations in which their relationship can grow, such as a Bible study or a class, pro-life work, youth work, or a ministry to the homeless. They can deepen friendships with each other's families by sharing in baptisms, funerals, birthdays, and reunions; double dating with you or with married siblings; attending siblings' performances (music or sports); or baby-sitting siblings' children.

Encourage young adults to maintain their other friendships and build new ones, particularly with other couples. Perhaps they can get involved in a couples' sports team or Bible study. They can invite friends over for dinner, games, or a movie.

Explore compatibility. Tests are available for discerning personality types and temperaments. Encourage the couple to take advantage of these and then to consider: Do the test results ring true? What insights do they give for possible challenges? Sharing at deeper levels leads to greater understanding of self, of what draws them to one another, and of what frustrates them about one another.

Encourage the couple to consider the cultural, economic, racial, or age similarities and dissimilarities they have. What influence does their birth order make, if any? Do they understand the love languages, and can they identify each other's? Opposites attract but can have challenging marriages. The couple needs time and maturity to recognize these differences and determine if the difficulties can be overcome.

Share convictions. The couple should share their perspectives on things that matter to them.

What are their financial goals? How do they approach debt? Do they follow a budget? Do they use credit cards, and if so, how do they avoid misuse?

What about children? Are they open to life? What do they think about Natural Family Planning? What is important to them in raising children?

Encourage the couple to enjoy each other in the midst of exploring their relationship and not to overanalyze each other. As my mother says, if you keep pulling up a plant by its roots to see if it is growing, you will kill it.

Safeguard purity. Time alone, even in prayer, can make couples more vulnerable to temptation, especially as they bare their souls. Some couples have shared that the only time they fell into sexual sin immediately followed an intense prayer time together. Other couples shared how they prayed near others as a way to limit their vulnerability.

Being alone in a secluded place is a way to court disaster rather than love. Time alone after midnight is particularly challenging. Tiredness and alcohol lower inhibitions.

Encourage the couple to set limits together and strengthen each other's resolve for purity. It takes two! Intense longing for each other could indicate love *or* lust. "Love is patient.... Love does not insist on its own way" (see 1 Corinthians 13:4, 5); but lust is not satisfied. Self-control (chastity) before marriage strengthens the foundation of faithfulness (chastity) in marriage.

It is important that the couple avoid near occasions of sin and demonstrate respect toward each other at all times. "We somehow think a godly Christian is one who can preheat the oven without cooking the roast."[1] Does the couple drive one another to Confession—meaning go with one another—or "drive" one another there due to immoral actions?

How do they feel after a date? If they feel joy, courtship is progressing well. If they feel guilt, sadness, or even remorse, something is wrong. Encourage them to reassess the relationship and reclaim a sense of peace. If they cannot, it is advisable to either pull back or pull out. Prolonging the inevitable may lead to confusion, poor decision making, and a lot of pain for both.

Guard the woman's natural virtue of hope. God has placed within women a natural virtue of hope. That is the reason women stay in port, keeping the home fires burning, while men go to sea. This is the positive side of this virtue, which contributes to marriages lasting longer than they might otherwise.

The negative aspect of this virtue is that women can hang on to hope based on mere threads of commitment, even in courting situations. The man should guard a woman's heart. If she is not the one for him, then he is not the one for her.

I remember feeling frustrated if a guy I dated had not called in a while. "Dad, why doesn't he call or come over? I don't understand what's going on!"

Dad would sigh, realizing he had to do the dirty work because this cowardly young man could not face me. "Yes, you do, honey."

"No, I really don't."

"Honey, he is not calling or coming over because he does not like you."

I would feel crushed. I knew Dad was telling me the truth. I had to let go of those feelings. Someday I would thank God that that relationship fell through.

If you have a son who hopes to reclaim a simple friendship following a breakup, caution him to rebuild slowly. He must allow time for healing, or he risks breaking her heart all over again. Reestablishing a friendship is possible, but only if there is a separation first. Like a GPS system that needs time to recalculate from a new position, a couple has to find a new route back to friendship.

On the other hand, if you know a young man who knows *who* his vocation is but remains single from fear, challenge him to get on with it. *She* is his path to sanctity! Sometimes it takes a little maternal (or paternal) kick in the pants to make a young man take responsibility for his vocation.

I shared this at a summer conference. A young man in attendance took my words to heart. He had the ring, but he had postponed proposing three times. After praying in the chapel, he went home and made flight reservations for the next day, to join his intended at her family reunion. And in front of her entire extended family, he proposed. They are happily married now, with eight children.

Be accountable. A courting couple values the input of key adults in their lives—parents, a mentor couple, a priest, older siblings. These adults are accountability partners who encourage the couple, offering wisdom and insight. "Where there is no guidance, a people falls; but in an abundance of counselors there is safety" (Proverbs 11:14).

These counselors provide layers of safety as a couple discern the most important decision of their lives. The counselors' role is not to tell the couple what to do but to be support staff, good listeners, advocates, and advisers. "Without counsel plans go wrong, but with many advisers they succeed" (Proverbs 15:22). Since marriage is a vocation in the Church, a priest or spiritual director should be one of those key advisers.

Consider timing. It could be time for engagement, or it could be the right person but the wrong time.

As I returned to Grove City College for my senior year, I found my heart very drawn to Scott Hahn. I did not want my heart to get ahead of our growing friendship, so I asked the Lord repeatedly to purify my desires. "Take delight in the LORD, and he will give you the desires of your heart. Commit your way to the LORD; trust in him, and he will act" (Psalm 37:4–5). I wanted my desires to conform to God's, even if that meant *not* being with Scott.

Finally, during a Young Life leaders' retreat in Laurelville, Pennsylvania, I sat alone on a rock and prayed, "Lord, either take away these desires or give me what I want!" I know that was a bold prayer, but I had relinquished my desires many times, and they had not diminished.

I left the rock and walked toward the conference room, and whom should I run into but Scott Hahn! He asked me if I wanted to take a walk with him. (Could he hear my pounding heart?) I quietly said I would, and we walked through the woods to a waterfall.

Scott let me know that he was thinking a lot about me and asked if I was interested in a long-term relationship.

"How long-term?" I asked.

"Maybe very long-term," he replied.

"I'd really like that," I responded, as calmly as I could. I even thought, If he asked me to marry him right now, I would say yes.

Months later Scott confided that he had almost asked then. Little did I know that he had already told others he was going to date me to marry me!

God has a plan for each of our lives, and it will unfold at the right time. We must trust him for the timing as well as the person, if that plan includes marriage.

QUESTIONS TO ASK BEFORE ENGAGEMENT

Here are some questions young people can ask to discern if engagement is right for them now.

- Is the Lord at the center of our relationship? It takes three to get married!

- Does our love reflect the description of love in 1 Corinthians 13:4–8?
- Do we understand and embrace the Catholic vision for marriage and family?
- Are we both ready to commit to all that the wedding vow means?
- For the guy: Am I ready to lead and to serve her? Can I provide for a wife?
- For the gal: Am I ready to follow his leadership? Can I care for a husband?
- Is our relationship growing in every way?
- Have we dealt with any complications from past relationships?
- Are our emotions based on reality?
- Do we have a growing sense of peace?
- Can we see ourselves growing old with each other?
- Can we do more for Christ together than separately?
- Do our accountability partners affirm that we are right for one another?

If the answers to these questions are yes, the next question is one of timing. Urge the couple to avoid long engagements. As parents we know what the young couple does not: Engagement will intensify their feelings and desires, creating a greater challenge to chastity than ever. Our guidance is critical. If a couple does not plan to marry for a long time, encourage a longer courtship rather than a lengthy engagement, or help them think through an earlier wedding date.

It is very important that a young man ask the father of his beloved (or mother, if there is no father available) for her hand in marriage. By doing this he acknowledges the privilege and responsibility God gave this father to raise his daughter. The young man honors her father by asking for the privilege and responsibility of being her husband.

One father asked, "Young man, are you ready to support a family?"

"Sir, I'm ready to support your daughter, but I'm afraid the rest of you will have to fend for yourselves!"

We smile, but from the father's standpoint, there are serious issues to discuss. "Give a daughter in marriage; you will have finished a great task. But give her to a man of understanding" (Sirach 7:25). Does this young man understand this is for life? Does he value the Church's teaching on marriage, including openness to life? This may be the father's one chance to make sure his future son-in-law "gets it."

CHAPTER NINE

Engagement Is a Time of Transition

Engagement is a whole new stage of a relationship. It is the time when a couple transition from their parents' orbit to establish their core. Though newlyweds will not jettison to a separate universe, their parents will recede to their periphery. Consequently, this is a time of transition for the families as well as the couple.

At this point our family includes fiancées in family photos and on family vacations. We give them gifts for their birthdays and Christmas, though not yet as much as a son or daughter. (Following the wedding we do not differentiate between our children and our sons- or daughters-in-law in gift-giving.) At the same time we welcome each son's or daughter's fiancé(e) into our family, we acknowledge ways the couple is differentiating from our family.

ENGAGEMENT IS A TIME OF PEACE

The guessing games are over—the *ifs* have become *whens.* Your son or daughter now knows *that* he or she will get married and *whom* he or she will marry. Each has chosen a beloved and been chosen. Now they can prepare for their life together!

For the young man this sense of resolution will be accompanied by a growing sense of responsibility.

A couple days after Scott proposed, I spotted him in the lobby of his dorm. He looked as if the weight of the world was on his shoulders.

"Scott, what's wrong?"

"I'm engaged," he said quietly, looking very pensive.

"Is that a bad thing?" I could hardly believe I was asking, but I needed to know.

"How will I feed you?" he asked in all seriousness.

I wanted to tease him by telling him I could feed myself. I also thought of saying that God would provide for us. I wanted to save him from feeling overwhelmed, but I knew this sense of responsibility was God-given.

First, God was the one who had called Scott to provide as a husband. Second, God was the one whom Scott needed to trust for that provision. (And God has provided through Scott's labor for more than thirty years.) It was humbling for Scott to realize how much more he had to depend on the Lord to provide through him for us. Scott's sense of peace increased the more he prayed with thanksgiving for God's provision.

ENGAGEMENT IS A TIME OF ANTICIPATION

Bridal magazines' timetables make it seem as if you need at least a year and thousands of dollars to plan a wedding. Take what is helpful; ignore what is not. Many people have been wed for much less money and in less time.

As parents of an engaged son or daughter, you remain a significant source of affirmation and support. Your interaction is part of their marriage preparation. Encourage the couple to meet with their pastor and begin the marriage preparation required by their diocese. (With few exceptions, the Church requires an engagement period of six months to a year, depending on the diocese, for marriage preparation.) Offer them a copy of *Chosen and Cherished: Biblical Wisdom for Your Marriage*, with specific questions for engaged couples in Appendix C.

ENGAGEMENT IS A TIME FOR GROWING IN LOVE

After an eighteen-month engagement, just six weeks prior to their wedding date, a couple I know canceled their wedding. The invitations were stamped; her wedding dress hung in the closet. They knew they loved each other, but they no longer felt in love. No use going through the motions and ending up with an unsatisfying marriage, they thought.

I shared Gary Chapman's *The Five Love Languages* with the woman. Was it possible that during this lengthy engagement they had stopped speaking each other's primary love language? Maybe he no longer had quality time for her because he was juggling a job and extra classes so they could get married. Perhaps the little time they had together she spent criticizing him for not being available instead of affirming his sacrifices.

The concept made sense. She immediately bought Gary Chapman's book and read it, then asked her fiancé to read it. A week later I saw them at the chapel. She was beaming; the diamond ring was on her finger again. The wedding was on!

Years later the husband thanked me. "I would have missed the love of my life!"

ENGAGEMENT IS A TIME OF CELEBRATION

It is easy to celebrate when a couple do things in the right order. As the mother or mother-in-law-to-be of the bride, you will most likely be invited to a bridal shower. Depending on the etiquette in your area, either a friend will offer to give a bridal shower or you will host one. Though your friends may not yet be her friends, they will want to celebrate with you. More than gifts, you want to shower the couple with love, prayers, and support.

Bridal showers are pro-life events, affirming marriage and family life. Consequently I invite the bride's relatives and friends, including their daughters (no matter how young), and the extended family and friends of the mother and mother-in-law who can attend. We play some games before opening gifts. We share a word of wisdom or a Scripture passage as the bride opens our gift. This keeps the focus on the bride, involves the givers more directly, and discourages the distracting private conversations that can dominate.

After the gifts are opened, we pray over the bride. Sometimes we sing the Doxology at the end. That has been a very meaningful way to celebrate the work of God in bringing the couple together.

ENGAGEMENT IS A TIME OF PREPARATION

Adam and Eve are the only married couple without parents, yet Genesis 2:24 states, "Therefore, a man leaves his father and his mother and clings to his wife, and they become one flesh." This has been an essential principal of marriage from the beginning, rather than an afterthought. Let's look briefly at each element.

Prepare to leave. In engagement our son or daughter prepares to leave our family home to make a home with a spouse. Our role as parents at this time is critical: "Preparation for marriage is of prime importance. The example and teaching given by parents and families remain the special form of this preparation" (*CCC,* 1632).

At the same time our role as parents is changing. We are becoming sideline support staff—available for advice but mostly waiting to be asked. We want to give the couple the relational space they need for making decisions about their future. If we affirm their independence, they will not feel the need to declare it. We honor the couple by loosening parental ties so they can "tie the knot" tighter.

The saying goes, "A son is a son until he has a wife; a daughter's a daughter for the rest of her life." This refers to the tendency of a young man to be closer to his family until he marries, while a young woman maintains more of a tender attachment to her family even after she marries.

During engagement both man and woman prepare to forge a new family, leaving their family of origin without disconnecting from them. Secondarily, they help each other foster closer ties to their families through this new relationship as a family within each family.

Prepare to cleave. To cling is to cleave: The couple prepares to join their lives. They plan for their life together without living together. They work on communication skills and deal with some frustrations without the intensity of life together. They make many decisions apart from parents, but not yet all. They craft a budget without merging bank accounts and paying bills. And they anticipate being united physically, with a date when that longing will be satisfied.

Parents address the future, couple to couple, offering "their children judicious advice, particularly when they are planning to start a family" (*CCC,* 2230). We affirm our love and loyal support for them and our confidence that the Lord will lead them. We assure them of our prayers, allowing them to share specific requests when they want.

There is a fine line between serving your fiancé(e) and becoming a servant. The saying "Happy wife, happy life" might imply that the man should do whatever it takes to make his bride-to-be or wife happy. That short-sells virtue. Both fiancés should please but not placate the other. They should serve each other with sacrificial love in holiness, so that both can say, "*Holy* spouse, *happy* house."

Prepare to become one flesh. For some couples, adjusting to life as newlyweds may not be a serious reason to abstain during times of fertility; for others it is. All couples should be trained in Natural Family Planning (NFP) during engagement, so they understand the rationale behind it, how the method works, and why it is so different from contraception. Couples who have been closed to the Church's teaching on life might become open. Whether or not couples intend to use NFP themselves, the information is useful: They can help other couples understand how to avoid (temporarily) or achieve pregnancy.

Couples continue to guard each other's chastity. As the big date approaches, they might benefit from reading Christopher and Rachel McCluskey's book *When Two Become One.*[1] It contains detailed information on marital intimacy that is best read shortly before the wedding.

NO COHABITATION

Even Christian parents have caved in to our culture by allowing their young adults to cohabit. One mother said, "I just hope they marry before they have a child."

No! As parents we *have* to do better than hope their immorality ends before children are involved. We must continue to parent our adult children by speaking the truth in love. We have the right and the responsibility to address this issue directly for the health and well-being of our young adults and their future. Here are some crucial thoughts we can share.

Cohabitation is "freedom" without responsibility. This is the very opposite of love. Blessed Pope John Paul II wrote in his Letter to Families: "'Free love' exploits human weaknesses; it gives them a certain 'veneer' of respectability with the help of seduction and the blessing of public opinion.... But not all of the consequences are taken into consideration, especially when the ones who end up paying are, apart from the other spouse, the children, deprived of a father or mother and condemned to be in fact orphans of living parents."[2]

That is a powerful and sad thought: "orphans of living parents."

You cannot "practice" a sacrament. Cohabitation does not reduce the divorce rate. Many couples who cohabit never marry. Of those cohabiting couples who do marry, they are more likely to divorce than couples who did not cohabit. Why? Marriage is a sacrament; you cannot practice a sacrament.

We should call cohabitation what it is: fornication! Sex outside of marriage is mortal sin. Getting the couple to Mass is not the solution, unless they have gone to Confession. (If they receive the Eucharist in the state of mortal sin, that is additional mortal sin.) They deserve the truth from their parents and their pastor.

A beloved should contribute to the other's sanctity—his or her path to heaven—before marriage and after. Leading each other into mortal sin is taking one another down the path to hell. This is not love!

Avoid the appearance of evil. Each couple is to "abstain from every form of evil" (1 Thessalonians 5:22) and avoid the appearance of evil. Do they avoid the near occasion of sin (limit temptations), making purity more possible? Do they distrust themselves? Are they committed to safeguarding their fiancé(e)'s virtue?

A couple might claim they are not having sex but are cohabiting just to save money. Do their neighbors, friends, and siblings know that? Even if a couple cohabits without fornicating, their example could lead weaker-willed couples to cohabit and fall sexually.

Many couples who approach the Church to get married are already cohabiting. A parish in Kansas addresses this as part of its marriage preparation class. The second week the class leader explains the Church's teaching on sex and openness to life and urges couples who are cohabiting to make a fresh start. Priests are there for Confession. And if the couple truly cannot afford two apartments, parish families are present to offer one of them a place, free of charge, until the wedding date. This is a parish committed to helping marriages succeed.

Stand firm with tough love. Stay united with your spouse. Do not allow your young adult to divide and conquer the two of you. Do not allow the couple to visit you with the expectation that they will share a room. And let them know *they* are the ones putting *you* in an awkward situation, not you them!

Affirm how much you want to see their future marriage thrive, not just survive. Be clear: Your rule is rooted in love for them. You want their best.

Preparing for the Mother-in-Law Dance

Life-changing for all. Just when you get the hang of being a family—toddlers and teens sleeping through the night, enjoying maturing friendships among siblings—life changes. You do not know what your expectations are for a child's engagement until it happens. There is great joy as your family expands. Your son or daughter now knows his or her vocation, the answer to many prayers. You now have the possibility of grandchildren.

Surprisingly there is also a sense of loss, even mourning, because things will never be the same. Your identity as the mother or father of this child does not change, but your relationship is now secondary to the relationship with his or her beloved. Many of your parental responsibilities now shift to the couple.

Though circumstances change, God never changes. Trust him with the changes, so that you can receive new gifts from him. You must let go in order to grasp something new.

Many friends who are mothers-in-law advised me, "Fade into the background," "Shut up and wear tan," and, "Back off." How was it possible for me to go from being the most significant woman in this child's life to being a person of no consequence? That characterization seemed too extreme. I did not want to be intrusive, but being told to back off seemed hurtful and negative. There had to be a better explanation of this transition than what my friends offered.

The analogy of dancing transformed this advice. If someone teaches you a dance step saying, "Step back," it is a simple direction. It is neutral—nothing hurtful or negative. You step back so there is room for someone else to step forward. The Mother-in-Law Dance is a difficult dance step, but engagement gives us time to practice. The more graciously we step back—and the sooner—the more easily the young couple can advance and invite us to come closer.

This analogy came to me independently of Annie Chapman's book, *The Mother-in-Law Dance: Can Two Women Love the Same Man and Still Get Along?*[3] Once I read her book, I appreciated this analogy even more. With the psalmist I can say, "You have turned my mourning into dancing; you have loosed my sackcloth and clothed me with gladness, that my soul may praise you and not be silent. O LORD my God, I will give thanks to you for ever" (Psalm 30:11–12).

Refine the art of interpretation. Each fiancé(e) needs to interpret his or her family to the beloved and the beloved to his or her family. Misunderstandings happen. We do not yet have a history on which to draw, and people may or may not be who they seem. We need to work on communication skills for the good of all involved. We ask our son or daughter for help in the translation process, and then we extend our trust, believing the best of each person.

The bride's family can feel overwhelmed with expenses and decisions, especially if the groom's family seems aloof or critical. The groom's family can feel as if they are being invited to their child's wedding instead of being included in the process, especially if the bride's family is not very communicative. Both sets of parents and the young couple should carefully weigh the sometimes conflicting advice of friends. Additionally, there are American customs, ethnic traditions, and Catholic norms to understand, as well as preferences of the couple and their parents. All of this leaves plenty of room for confusion.

We all have expectations, hopes, and dreams that we may not even fully understand ourselves. We pray for wisdom and insight. We ask the Holy Spirit to interpret each of us to the others, so that we might have the kind of extended family that demonstrates love and grace in action.

Prepare More for the Marriage Than for the Wedding

Focus on a great marriage. The wedding is one amazing day but *only* one day. Marriage lasts a lifetime. The plans can become all-consuming during the limited time a couple has to be together during engagement. Will they use some of that time to grow closer rather than just reviewing wedding to-do lists? Parents can help a couple focus on priorities, or they can exacerbate the imbalance by adding pressure about the wedding day.

A newly married friend said, with a straight face, "No matter how bad it gets, it will get better!"

I did not know what to say. She was the only daughter of a well-to-do couple. Though she had married a man of meager means, she had wanted a spare-no-expense gala, and her parents could provide it. What his family could not afford, her parents spent, so that everything was done "right." The focus of their engagement had been the extravaganza.

"My wedding day was the day of my dreams," she continued. "Three days later I came to a horrible realization: I'm just cleaning toilets for the rest of my life!" She was unprepared for the sacrificial life of marriage, and her parents did her no favor by providing for her what her new spouse could not.

A few years later the marriage ended in divorce. I am convinced the seeds for that divorce were planted and nurtured during their engagement.

Honor all involved. As a Presbyterian pastor, my dad had married hundreds of couples. He recommended that Scott and I consider family members first for our bridal party, though we might feel closer to some friends. Over the years we might not see friends much, but we would gather with family at least once a year. If we honored family members now, we could strengthen our relationships for years to come. This was great advice.

"Love does not insist on its own way; it is not irritable or resentful" (1 Corinthians 13:5). This is a helpful dictum for all parties involved in a wedding. If we demand our way, we lose. If we are deferential, we all win.

Avoid debt. What is essential for a wedding? Some families take a second mortgage on their home to give their child a dreamed-of wedding, but at what cost? The wedding is only one day—though admittedly one of the most important in a couple's life. When the bills roll in after the big day, will the couple wish they had spent less money so that there was more in the bank for their life together?

A wedding budget is very important. Pray for creative options so you can avoid debt. Be mindful of the costs for dresses and tuxes, especially for married friends. Pray before you shop. I shared the details in *Chosen and Cherished* about how my sisters and I purchased the wedding dress that all three of us wore. This is not to suggest that you share a wedding gown, but are there corners you can cut?

Carefully consider what matters to you and to each set of parents, rather than letting bridal magazines' lists dictate costs. What will matter twenty years from now, and what will not? Photos can only be taken on the wedding day, but is a limousine optional? Could the ring bearer use an inexpensive suit he can wear again, rather than a matching tuxedo rented for one day?

Are there creative options for flowers? Gabriel and Sarah saved money on the table arrangements for the reception. Her family purchased vases they could use at future weddings; friends arranged the flowers. The result was stunning.

Michael and Ana ordered fresh flowers for Ana and made the bridesmaids' bouquets with silk flowers months beforehand, at a fraction of the cost of real flowers. The photos revealed no difference between the silk and the real flowers; all were beautiful.

Sometimes people offer their labor as a wedding gift. They will make the cake, if you pay for the ingredients. Or they will arrange the flowers for the church, or make corsages and boutonnières, if you pay for the flowers. Perhaps a friend who is a photographer or a videographer will offer that labor (though you may prefer a professional). You can cut expenses without limiting the joy of the day.

Be inclusive when it comes to celebrations during the week of the wedding. Can the two families gather for an informal afternoon at a zoo or a park the day before other guests arrive? Can grandparents and other relatives join siblings and friends for fun, creative bachelor or bachelorette parties?

How can the groom's (or bride's) family offer hospitality to family and friends if the wedding is out of town? Sometimes a hotel offers a room for a gathering space, where you can have food and drinks, board games, and photo albums. If there are several hours between the wedding and the reception, perhaps friends in the area can make their home available for a gathering. For out-of-town guests, consider placing in their rooms gift bags with various snack foods, bottles of water, and holy cards as reminders to pray for the couple getting married.

Can the priest offer a time for Confession, especially for the bridal party? "It is…appropriate for the bride and groom to prepare themselves for the celebration of their marriage by receiving the sacrament of penance" (*CCC,* 1622). Gabriel and Sarah requested Confession be available during a holy hour following the rehearsal dinner. It was a wonderful time for preparing our hearts and minds for the following day. This may not be convenient for your wedding, given the hour of the wedding or the distance of the church from the rehearsal dinner. Whatever you do, let it bring peace rather than stress.

If non-Catholic family members or friends attend the wedding, can you include notes in the wedding program explaining the liturgy so they can follow along more easily? Assume people want to participate, and ask how you can facilitate that. It is also helpful to note in the program or through the priest that only Catholics in good standing can receive Communion.

The Wedding Day

Everyone is ready! On the wedding day, all is in a state of readiness for the bride to be presented to the groom. Have you ever noticed that the passage following St. Paul's lengthiest teaching on marriage (see Ephesians 5:21–6:4) is his lengthiest teaching on spiritual warfare (Ephesians 6:10–18)? This is not an accident. The world is a battleground, and our marriages and families are under attack.

Did you know that other Scriptures refer to being "ready" almost exclusively in battle lingo? Here is a quick list: ready to arm, ready to go into battle, ready to perish, ready to breach, ready to go, ready to depart, ready to preach, ready to give an answer for the faith, ready to be offered, and ready to die. These passages remind us of the connection between holiness and spiritual warfare.

The couple is ready to depart on their adventure of marriage, to preach to the world and give an answer for their faith with their lives, especially as they are open to life. They are ready to offer themselves to and for each other, to die to themselves and to live for Christ. They remind us, "For though we live in the world we are not carrying on a worldly war" (2 Corinthians 10:3).

As I watched our children marry, I was overwhelmed by their desire for a marriage and family that honor God. By declaring their intent, they knew they now had bull's-eyes on their backs. A marriage established in faithful, holy love *is* an assault on the kingdom of darkness by the kingdom of light. As parents we must be prayer warriors on our children's behalf as they face challenges.

135

They will experience conflict. Some struggles will be simply the human challenges of learning how to live well together. Others will be spiritual conflicts, because *this* marriage is a target for the Evil One. Satan prowls the earth to destroy what is good and holy, if he can.

What God inspires—and what Satan desires—is the next generation. Our prayers and words of wisdom fortify them so they can stand, side by side, fully armed for the battle that lies ahead. As Jesus promised, "I have said this to you, that in me you may have peace. In the world you have tribulation; but be of good cheer, I have overcome the world" (John 16:33).

Mass is a fitting context for the sacrament of matrimony. A father walked his daughter down the aisle, paused, and then spoke quietly to the couple. When he sat down, his wife asked, "What did you say?"

"I told them, '*This* is the moment. Focus. Don't miss it!'" What a loving reminder at the critical moment the Mass was beginning.

When we attend a Christian wedding, we witness a miracle. A man and a woman administer the sacrament to one another before the Church, pledging their free consent. The two are bound as one.

Why do we celebrate weddings at Mass? "It is therefore fitting that the spouses should seal their consent to give themselves to each other through the offering of their own lives by uniting it to the offering of Christ for his Church made present in the Eucharistic sacrifice, and by receiving the Eucharist so that, communicating in the same Body and the same Blood of Christ, they may form but 'one body' in Christ" (*CCC,* 1621).

Christ, the Bridegroom of our souls, gives himself to us, his bride, in the Eucharist. In marriage we give ourselves to each other in life-giving love. We imitate Christ's sacrificial love in our sacramental marriage; we hope it will be fruitful.

As we witnessed the young couple's vows, *we* knew how hard it would be—and how beautiful—for them to live the magnitude of their consent. While they were establishing the core relationship of their marriage in Christ, Scott and I were moving into the background, with a less immediate but no less important role. For the rest of our lives we would have the privilege of undergirding this new family with our love and support.

The reception is a couple's first act of hospitality. Sarah framed their reception as their first act of hospitality, facilitated by her parents. What a beautiful gesture to describe the reality of their unity immediately following the wedding. And it provided an outward focus from the beginning of their marriage.

Let the honeymoon be a time for rest and relaxation. Some people take an expensive vacation for their honeymoon. Some even delay their wedding so they can afford such a vacation. If a couple have saved themselves sexually for marriage, they do not need a lot of activities. They will have vacations for the rest of their life.

Most young couples cannot imagine how exhausted they will be after the wedding. Now is the time to revel in what God has revealed and be alone to express love to one another. I suggest a bed-and-breakfast close by, if possible, with some bath oil beads, some good wine and good music. The honeymoon is a time to enjoy each other and begin a wonderful life together with Christ at the center.

PART FIVE

…Her Husband Also,

and He Praises Her

—Proverbs 31:28

CHAPTER TEN

The Mother-in-Law Dance

Not only do the children of the Proverbs 31 woman praise her; "her husband also, and he praises her" (Proverbs 31:28b). He acknowledges ways she has helped their children mature to adulthood. He shares her joy as they watch their children become husbands and fathers, wives and mothers. This is an amazing time of growth in their family's life.

When we began this series in 2006, none of our children was married. As of 2011 we have added two daughters-in-law, four granddaughters, and another grandchild is on the way. We have gained seven new family members in four years. That is significant growth!

We have new kinds of relationships. Moms often facilitate relationships. We help each family member get a sense of his or her place in the family vis-à-vis other family members. We have new roles: Scott and I are now father- and mother-in-law and grandparents. Our children have become sisters- and brothers-in-law, aunts and uncles.

In Hebrew the word for "father-in-law" means "circumciser." This may be why there are no father-in-law jokes. Seriously, there seem to be far fewer conflicts with fathers-in-law than with mothers-in-law.

When I tried to find a mother-in-law joke, I was appalled; every one I found was mean or vicious. Perhaps some women contribute to the stereotype. However, my mom and my mother-in-law have been wonderful examples of the love that is possible in an in-law relationship.

In-law relationships can be complicated through divorce. Some people have two sets of in-laws. Or you could be the second set of in-laws if your child marries someone who has been divorced. A different complication arises with cohabitation—when a mother-in-law is *not* a mother-in-law. Should you treat your child's "significant other" like family, even though the couple are not married and might never marry? It is all catawampus.

When I looked for resources on in-law relationships, I found almost nothing! And this is an area for which many families would like some wisdom. So let's take a fresh look at the beautiful relationship that is *possible* and *desirable* between in-laws.

A RENEWED VISION

Christians present to the world a very different view of marriage and family life. We can also present a very different picture of in-law relationships.

We are the bride of Christ, Christ is the Groom, and Mary is the mother of the Groom. If the groom's mother is the mother-in-law, then in some sense, Mary is the mother-in-law of the Church. If anyone can redeem that relationship, it is Mary. She is a reflection of what God desires us to be as mothers-in-law. Like Mary, will we support, nurture, and love unconditionally our in-laws? Will we wait to be welcomed into an in-law's heart, not imposing ourselves but responding to an invitation for a close relationship?

As with any meaningful relationship, we need time for it to develop naturally. Though I am a seasoned daughter-in-law, I am still learning to communicate my love for my mother-in-law and my gratitude for the gift of my husband. At the same time I am beginning to understand my role as a mother-in-law. I want to communicate the love in my heart in ways my in-laws can receive. By the grace of God, I am learning the dance steps of an "altared" relationship (pun intended). I hope you find them helpful.

Begin with joy! If you have a married child, congratulations! You have completed a leg of the journey in parenting your child. But you are not yet finished. Now you are ready for the next phase. Your son or daughter will not be dependent on you in the same way, but in a sense the circle of dependence is growing. You are still an essential part of God's plan. Just as you should anticipate a good relationship with your teens, anticipate a good relationship with the newly married couple. Your attitude is one of the keys for a good relationship.

A new relationship, a new name. Scott and I decided to call each other's parents Mom and Dad as soon as we greeted them after our wedding. Doing so was important to us, because this was a covenant for keeps. By the words we used, we acknowledged that we were really family. This was a way I could honor Scott's parents, and he mine.

I did not know what my mother-in-law thought about this until she heard Sarah greet me as Mom immediately following the wedding. She told Sarah, "I am so glad you and Gabe are going to call each other's parents Mom and Dad. I didn't do it at the beginning, and I was never able to after that."

Anyone in the world can refer to Mary. When I call her Mother Mary, I acknowledge her as my spiritual mother, and that opens up my heart more to her. Likewise, many people call me Kimberly, but only my children call me Mom.

We can give permission without pressure, leaving room for everyone's comfort level. Any change can be awkward. For instance, it would have seemed strange to have gone from calling my mother-in-law "Mrs. Hahn" to calling her "Lou," her first name.

Could there be a good reason *not* to use *Mom* and *Dad?* One woman said she loved her parents too much to share those names with anyone. I understand, but I wanted to extend to my in-laws the natural love I have for my parents, to honor them as my husband's parents. Saying so helped make it so.

I prefer the term *daughters-by-covenant* to *daughters-in-law*, because the law does not make me take them into my mother's heart, but the covenant really makes us family. Some people prefer *daughter-* or *son-in-love*. Whatever the term, let's define our new relationship positively.

A new relationship, a new last name. Wives take their husband's last name as an expression of family unity and a sign that he is the head of the family. Our children receive *our* family name. St. Paul says, "For this reason I bow my knees before the Father, from whom every family in heaven and on earth is named" (Ephesians 3:14).

Some women fear identity loss should they change their last name, but they already have a last name from a man—their father—*and* they have their own identity. Others say divorce is simpler if a woman does not change her last name, but how sad to make a decision assuming divorce. Rather, as Catholics, we assume an indissoluble bond through marriage as we form a new family with our husband, united under one family name.

A new relationship, a new patron saint? I want a close, meaningful relationship with each in-law. What better way to elicit assistance than petition the patron saint of in-laws? So I looked through more than four thousand saints on the Vatican website. *No one* is designated for in-laws! That may be the biggest oversight in the universe.

Any saint will pray for us, but I would like to have a chosen champion. There are saints who weathered tough relationships with in-laws and who could be great guides, like St. Rita of Cascia and St. Frances of Rome.

Enlarge the circle. Sometimes people say, "You aren't losing a son but gaining a daughter" (or vice versa). Maybe, maybe not. It can become true if we develop a relationship that is built on trust, mutual respect, and love, but it is not automatic.

What has your relationship with your mother-in-law been like? You may carry baggage into this new relationship with your child's spouse (just as your mother-in-law might have carried some). If you hope to make up for shortcomings and unmet needs or desires, you may cause an imbalance with a new in-law. If it seems as if nothing was lacking in your relationship with your mother-in-law, you may be unprepared for potential challenges.

Naturally we are closer to our own child, but we open our heart to include his or her spouse. Our relationship changes into a mediated relationship with the two of them. If we try to maintain a closed circle—to hold our new in-law at arm's length—we will find that we are the ones left out of the circle. By God's design they are one. We need to draw our in-laws into our hearts, and there we will find our children.

Family forever. One day I realized something amazing: Sarah and Ana, as daughters-in-law, are more likely to be at my deathbed than my dearest sibling or friend. I want the kind of relationship beforehand that welcomes that precious time when it comes. Why not build a relationship in which we anticipate with delight the years to come? We do not want to put up with each other; we want to cherish each other.

How long did it take to get to know your child? For nine months you anticipated this child's entrance into the family. You had years of building trust and experiencing life together. And when you crossed wills, you usually won, being the parent.

With an in-law you might have very few months to build a relationship before you have to make life-changing decisions, occasionally crossing wills. You may not know this person well, but you know God has placed you in each other's lives to bless your family and to build his kingdom. You are to love without measure, regardless of return (see 1 John 3:18).

Include in-laws fully. The first birthday of our first daughter-in-law, we set the precedent of spending the same amount on her gifts as we would for our child. We do the same for Christmas gifts. By God's grace we have been joined in a unique relationship as in-laws. It is a privilege to include these women fully into our family.

A friend told me that she has never been included in a family photo, though her children routinely are. I am so sorry her husband did not draw the line the first time: Include her, or I step out of the photo.

Siblings' Friendships Thrive with Honor and Respect

For siblings "left behind" after the wedding. I spoke to a mother who recently found out that the day she married, her young siblings hid her car keys so she could not leave on her honeymoon. They cried when she found them. Twenty years later one of her sisters confessed deep bitterness for feeling abandoned and even asked her for forgiveness.

Siblings need to know they still matter. An engaged couple are focused on each other and wedding details. They are not thinking about a loss, because they are not losing. They do not regret leaving home; they are sailing off into the bright blue yonder with the love of their life.

But siblings may feel the loss of a close relationship. Young siblings may feel as if their newly married sibling is choosing a new family (as opposed to adding another family member and creating their own new family). They can feel this acutely when newlyweds settle closer to the other family. This is where mothers have a critical role, correcting misperceptions and sensitizing siblings to each other's concerns.

The more an engaged couple includes siblings in their plans, the better. Asking them to be a part of the bridal party is great, but is there anything else they can do? Can the couple include a sibling on errands, enjoy a shake together, or attend the sibling's game or concert? Simple efforts can dispel a younger sibling's concerns about still being important.

Gabriel spent his last night as a single man at the hotel with his brothers. Michael spent his last night as a single man at home. It was great for both of them to gather with their siblings before the momentous founding of their own families.

After the wedding, especially if the couple is in a hurry, they may find it difficult to say individual good-byes to siblings. Try to facilitate the farewells if you can. Small acts of kindness from the newlyweds can keep wounds from forming.

Questions on a sibling's heart after the wedding are, Am I still important to them? Will they remember my birthday? Will they still give me a Christmas present? Will they call? If money is tight and newlyweds live far from one of their families, they might not be able to afford a trip home for Christmas. They might not have money for gifts to send home either. How does a sibling at home interpret this?

Is it possible for us to budget travel money—for gas or plane tickets—for our married children? Can we make it possible for a sibling to visit the couple? Reuniting newlyweds with their siblings is important in keeping them close and establishing a relationship with the new in-law. If two or three years pass between visits, gaps in relationships can form that may be difficult to bridge. They can close their hearts to each other.

We should not manipulate our children into coming home, spending vacations with us, or even attending celebrations of sacraments or birthdays. We make decisions for our unmarried children at home and invite our married children to join us. We respect our married children's decisions to establish their own traditions, which may or may not include coming home for the holidays.

For siblings who wed. The child who just married comes home wondering, What is my place in the family, and where does my spouse fit in? New relationships need to be forged. Honor and respect are important to everyone.

Older siblings want to remain in their younger siblings' circles of influence, even if they live far away. After months apart, older siblings need to make deposits into their younger siblings' emotional bank accounts, noticing the things they are doing well before they correct them. The more the older ones extend friendship, the more open the hearts of the younger ones will be to their advice. This is also true of in-laws with whom there is still a developing relationship. Sometimes in-laws recognize more quickly how much younger children have matured, because they have not known them as long.

Married couples have to reach out to the unmarried. When they come home for a visit, how can we strengthen their relationships? Maybe siblings can reconnect by going out for ice cream or playing a round of miniature golf. Can a spouse understand a sibling's need for time with a brother or sister, to renew and refresh the relationship, both one-on-one and as a couple?

One of our Christmas gifts to our children is ten dollars per person for a sibling date, including in-laws, varying who is paired each year. We agree on the day and time everyone will go for one to two hours. This is a small investment in relationships that will produce large dividends.

Blaze the trail. What example have we set for our children with our own siblings? Are we in touch? If we live far away, and we are the ones who have moved, do we make the effort to visit? Do we welcome them into our home? Do we contact them on a regular basis by phone or e-mail? Do we ever send gifts? What has helped us remain close provides a path for our children to follow as they become adults.

For more than thirty years of our married life, my parents have made it possible for us to vacation as an extended family. (For many years, had they not paid for a vacation, we would not have had one.) All we have to do is get there; they pay for everything—food, lodging, activities, and even spending money. The grandchildren, their spouses, and the great-grandchildren are included.

One of the highlights is family sharing for an hour each morning. We sing, led by the grandchildren who play instruments, we pray, and we share in a Bible study. We have forged strong friendships through prayer, fun in the sun, great meals, and one-on-one time.

SIBLINGS, SPEAK THE FIVE LOVE LANGUAGES POST-WEDDING

Look for ways to facilitate communication between your children. Encourage them to contact each other. Give them reminders about upcoming birthdays and anniversaries. Send gift request lists for Christmas. Take siblings to visit others, or send siblings to visit alone. Request a "good thing" of the week, via phone or e-mail, and share them with the family. (I also record each person's good thing for the week in a special journal.) Share prayer concerns.

The following are practical ways siblings can express their love to each other once one is married.

Words of affirmation—in person, by phone, or in notes:

- birthday card or note affirming something you appreciate about the sibling
- thank you-notes in response to gifts or visits
- calls to share good news

Gift giving—in person or by mail:
- collecting coupons or stickers; making homemade coupons with offers to serve
- shopping thoughtfully for gifts
- making gifts for one another
- getting gifts for loved ones when they receive sacraments

Quality time—in person or by phone:
- visits, allowing time for one-on-one conversations
- taking one another out for coffee or lunch
- regular phone calls
- participating in siblings' sacraments and birthdays

Acts of service—in person and through prayer:
- on visits, helping with studies, yard work, and projects
- offering Mass or a rosary for a sibling's intentions and letting the person know
- being a godparent to a niece or nephew and filling the role well

Physical touch (in person) and closeness (from afar):
- greeting each other with affection when you are together: hugs, kisses, high-fives, wrestling, pats on the back
- using Skype
- creating an online family newsletter to share everyone's good things of the week, prayer concerns, photos, and so on

We want our children to enjoy lifelong friendships with each other.

MAKE YOUR HOME THEIR HOME

How can your family home become a home for your daughter- or son-in-law? What blessed you when you went home to visit your parents or parents-in-laws?

Both my mom and my mother-in-law know how to make homes that are beautiful and tasteful, where I can rest and relax. They plan ahead and make delicious meals. They always set a beautiful table, with attention to the season or holiday. I try to imitate their gracious style. Here are six *P*s that help me prepare for a great time together:

Pray. Ask the Holy Spirit for creative touches that communicate love and thoughtfulness. Fresh flowers are probably not on a newlywed budget; can you place some in their room? If they arrive by plane, can you make a vehicle available to them for at least some of the time? Ask the Lord to guide you so that your new in-law feels at home. You want each time together to help you move beyond loving someone because he or she loves your child to loving someone you know.

Plan. Ask ahead if there is something they would like to do all together. Gather specifics to make it easier to plan a special outing. (What time is the facility open? How do you get there? What is the cost?) Invite each couple (if there is more than one) for breakfast or lunch, to catch up two-on-two. Are there games, movies, and puzzles in your home that people would enjoy, or can you purchase some? Post on the fridge daily Mass and Confession schedules for area churches or special Mass schedules around Christmas or Easter.

Prepare so as to communicate how much you have thought of each person.

Food. What are each person's favorite foods? Is anyone on a special diet or allergic to any foods? Are there meals that can be made ahead and frozen, to simplify preparation and free up time for you to be with everyone?

The better plan you have for meals, the simpler it is to feed a crowd. If your children live close and bring something for a meal, let them know their contribution is appreciated.

In warm weather you can pack a picnic lunch or dinner and have it at a park or in the backyard. If you have an activity planned, you may want to order pizza, pick up subs, or eat out.

If you want them to feel at home, establish an open-fridge policy. When people are hungry or thirsty, encourage them to help themselves.

Supplies. Place a basket of toiletries in the guest bathroom, including shampoo, conditioner, a new shaver, toothpaste, a new toothbrush, fingernail clippers, lotion, some Q-tips, and a clean comb. Stock a medicine cabinet with Tylenol, Advil, cold and flu pills, Airborne, Tums, and cough drops.

Comfort. Is there enough hot water for everyone to shower? (We increased the size of our hot water tank to accommodate our growing family.) Are the beds firm or soft enough? Are there enough pillows? Is anyone allergic to down in pillows or comforters? Is anyone allergic to family pets? (You may have to find another home for your pet.) Are bedrooms too cold, too hot, or too dry? Show everyone where you have extra blankets and pillows.

Illness. Illness can be a visit spoiler. The combination of early mornings, late nights, and not sleeping well, coupled with too much sugar and a mix of germs (with all of that huggin' and kissin'), amounts to increased risk of flu, colds, coughs, and sore throats. Minimize germs by having tissues on hand and spraying bathroom sinks and toilets daily with Lysol.

Limit clutter. Are there places to put purses, coats, and other winter paraphernalia? Do guest rooms have some dresser and closet space available so couples can unpack and feel settled? Is your home clean and orderly? Does it smell good?

Participate. How can you be available? How can you help your husband, who may be working during the visit, also have time with the couple? Set work aside, as much as you can, so they do not feel as if you are fitting them into your busy schedule.

My mother-in-law loves knitting, quilting, and other handcrafts. I used to bring a craft and sit with her in the family room, so we could talk while we stitched. We took walks together with the dog. She still enjoys walking, which is a great time for us to talk.

I am not territorial in my kitchen. I take any help I am offered, but I also enjoy giving young wives a break from cooking and serving meals. They can put up their feet and read a good book, take a nap, or sit in the kitchen and talk to me. Or they can help me, which is also a joy. I do appreciate help with cleanup from anyone who is willing.

Privacy. How can a couple have space alone in our home? Can they have a private bedroom and bathroom?

When we added space to our cabin, I asked the contractor to use his thickest insulation on the inside walls. He politely corrected me, "You mean exterior walls."

"Both exterior *and* interior walls," I replied. "I hope that when my married children stay at our cabin, they will have a sense of privacy in making love, not wondering if anyone can hear them. That's why I want the thickest insulation on the *interior* walls too."

The contractor smiled broadly. No one had requested that before, but he understood why I did and thought it was a good idea.

Peace. Remember, this visit is for a limited time. Offer up difficulties as an act of love, and you will gain graces for the whole family. Always have the humility to say, "How can we make the next visit better?" Everyone wants to help create special memories.

VISIT YOUR CHILDREN'S HOMES

Your married son or daughter will love showing you the home the couple has made, whether it be an apartment, a duplex, or a spacious house. When you are in their home, you get great ideas for gifts. You notice ways you can serve them. You have opportunities to affirm them, express affection, and have quality conversations. These expressions of love flow naturally when you are together; they are more difficult from a distance.

Offer to help in the kitchen. Take your cue from your daughter or daughter-in-law. Does she want your help with the cooking or with setting the table? Serve however she would like. Whatever you do, honor the kitchen as her territory, and *never* rearrange the cupboards!

How can you serve? Everything should be ordered to that end. What can you do to undergird rather than undermine your married children? To appreciate rather than be critical of them? If you have a good relationship, expressions of love are more easily interpreted as such: Blessed if you do, blessed if you don't. If you do not, your actions can be misinterpreted: Damned if you do, damned if you don't.

For instance, are frequent calls seen as caring or intrusive? Are infrequent calls seen as giving the couple space or not caring? Is sharing family members' accomplishments keeping us connected or making subtle comparisons and bragging? Is not sharing others' accomplishments being sensitive or intentionally withholding information? Is an unexpected gift a nice surprise or an effort to manipulate the couple and "show up" the other in-laws? Does a lack of gifts mean you cannot afford them or you do not care enough to buy them? If we work on a good relationship, our actions (and theirs) will be interpreted in the best possible light.

When you visit, do not speak poorly of any family member. Few things can tear down family relations faster than gossip. How we speak of others in their presence signals how we should speak of them in their absence.

It is a privilege to be invited to your child's home. Notice and appreciate the couple's efforts to serve you and to meet your needs while you are there. Send them a thank-you note after a visit, highlighting those efforts.

God, grant us the grace as an expanding family of families to continue to nurture meaningful relationships among our children.

CHAPTER ELEVEN

Newlyweds Forge a New Family

If newlyweds live near either (or both) family, it can be a mixed blessing. They can feel strengthened as a new family—living on their own but not feeling alone—provided they establish some boundaries. Parents must not intrude or intervene inappropriately. Otherwise they can stunt the growth of the couple as a new family.

Newlyweds must rely first on God and second on each other for problem solving, before they approach their parents. This will be a new pattern to establish. Their proximity to parents may make this a challenge.

It is best if newlyweds or their parents call before they stop by. That way everyone honors the independence of each family unit. Likewise, invitations must be invitations and not expectations; sometimes the invited may not choose to come. Given these boundaries, it can be a great blessing to live close to one or both families of origin.

If a couple does not live near parents, they must depend on each other. This is essential for a strong marriage, yet a couple who do not experience much support and encouragement from their families can feel isolated, lonely, and stressed. If parents stay in touch, though, the couple can still experience their support.

ESTABLISH TRADITIONS

Parents should not take it personally if newlyweds establish different traditions when it comes to birthdays, holidays, and vacations. We had the freedom to do what we wanted with our own family, and sadly, that time is passing. We can make suggestions or invitations, but it is important to honor the couple's decisions.

For many years Scott and I lived far from both of our families. We traveled to one family the week before Christmas and joined the other for the week after Christmas. One of my siblings asked when we would begin our own traditions. I replied, "We have. *This* is our tradition: We travel so that we spend this special holiday with both of our families."

Both the new husband and the new wife should share ideas from their families as they forge their traditions.[1] They will blend the traditions they find meaningful from each family and develop new ones.

Two families join at the point of the couple's unity, but those families do not blend. Rather, the couple forms a new family that is now a family within two families of families. We can enjoy each other and appreciate the love and care shown the couple by our son's or daughter's in-laws, but we are not one larger family with those in-laws.

It would get extraordinarily complicated to have close relationships with all of our children's in-law families, especially given our large family. Sometimes our families' paths will cross at a birthday party, a sacramental celebration, a graduation, or a wedding. We build friendships, especially when we share the faith, but we most likely will not vacation together or share holidays.

The natural tug of a new husband or wife is to spend time as a couple with one's own parents and siblings. Deeper bonds of unity occur for the couple when a wife draws her husband toward *his* family and a husband draws his wife toward *hers*. I made it a priority to be available and creative in how we could spend time with Scott's parents and siblings, and Scott made it a priority to help us enjoy time with my parents and siblings. This way neither of us was trying to convince the other to include our extended families. We pulled together instead of pulling away from each other. By drawing each other's hearts closer to our families of origin—in love, not dependence—we brought greater wholeness to our marriage.

This truth applies to me in two ways as a mother-in-law. I want to enjoy my children's spouses, and I want my children to enjoy being with their spouses' families. I will not participate in a tug-of-war between families. My goal is to strengthen their marriages by hosting them in our home *and* by encouraging time with in-laws. This will bring greater wholeness to each of their marriages and blessing to their children.

Family life is more about caring for each other than about rights. If a decision affects our larger family, we ask the married couples for input. That does not mean the married couples dictate what the larger family does. Nor does it mean the couples must do what the larger family does. We recognize they are independent families.

RISK LOVE

Love bears all things. When you were expecting, you wondered what your child would be like, but you did not wonder *if* you would like him or her. Once your child was born, you lavished your love without expecting a response for a long time. You spoke words of love your child did not understand and met needs he or she could not yet articulate. You loved without measure, without condition.

Being a good mom is your education in being a good mother-in-law. You lead with love without asking whether or not you like this man or woman. If you lavish love without expectation of how quickly it will be reciprocated, speaking words of love and meeting needs, you will be amazed. Your child's beloved will welcome you into his or her heart.

Love believes all things. Because you trust your child, you trust the person your child trusts. Still, there are natural limits to this trust, since you do not yet know this person well. Can there be a supernatural release of those limits? Can you risk beyond what you can see? Just as we do with our own children, we extend a line of credit to our daughters- or sons-in-law.

Initially we love this person because this person loves our child and is loved by our child. We receive this person as a gift, just as we received our child as a gift. We lavish unconditional love to build the foundation of love and trust we already enjoy with our child.

Love hopes all things. What happens when you disagree? It can surprise you, especially since misunderstandings and hurt feelings can happen before much time has passed. If you are mature men and women of God, why would you have conflict? Think about it: Do you ever disagree with your spouse? Your children? Yes!

You will have disagreements with your in-laws. It can feel disappointing, but do not let it be shattering. This is just human stuff. You will get through it.

As with our teens, I can only work on my side of the equation and extend forgiveness, whether or not it is requested. I can extend the line of credit again, even if trust has been broken. (This is also true of my in-law toward me.) I choose to anticipate a beautiful relationship, just as I do with our teens. I pray for a close and meaningful relationship, believing that is God's desire for us, though it may take time.

Just as we do not have a history with this new family member, so they do not yet know us well. Are we women of our word? Do we demonstrate trustworthiness in all things, big and little? If their friends or siblings have experienced strained relationships with in-laws, they may anticipate something similar with us. Likewise, we may have been influenced by others. We must resist the temptation to allow stereotypes to define our relationship and ask the Lord to remove whatever hinders positive in-law relationships. Then we find ways to express genuine love as women of integrity.

Sometimes we feel blindsided by misunderstandings. Some are minor; others may be more serious. Remember that well-meaning people with different opinions can have strong disagreements and still love each other.

Every family does not resolve conflict the same way. Typically, our family talks about keeping short accounts. We try to deal with conflicts when they occur, which sometimes is confrontational. Other families may internalize their feelings and think more before deciding what has to be resolved through conversation, which can cause strain. Sometimes people do not perceive conflicts where others do, or they may dread conflicts so much that they avoid them where possible and prefer to forgive without a lot of discussion. We cannot impose our way. Deep resolution is in God's hands, and we cannot force it.

I think this is a helpful word picture: We forge strong bonds of love like steel. It has to be heated and hammered in the right way, so that it does not become brittle and shatter. This will not be pain-free, but it does not have to be agonizing. St. Elizabeth Ann Seton's words are helpful: "Looking up steadily spares the pain, both of retrospection and anticipation."[2] The more we keep our eyes on Jesus, the more peace we will have.

Love endures all things. Trusting and waiting are not the same as doing nothing. There are times we feel helpless as parents. We cast our situation on the Lord and trust in him. We ask Mary to intercede for us; she can intervene where we cannot. This is a proactive and not passive response. And the Holy Spirit may inspire our imitation of Mary as we ponder what God is doing.

Any of us can demand our own way, but we know that is not the way of love. I realize that my perspective is limited, and my capacity for self-deception (seeing others' faults instead of my own) is staggering. I can put the best possible face on what I have said or done, while I put the worst face on what someone else has said or done. Then I react emotionally as if *that* is reality.

We have a lot to learn through our vocation as wife and mother (including being a mother-in-law). God is at work in us, and he will not be done with us for a long time.

PRAY THROUGH THE PAIN

Sometimes there will be relational strain with an in-law for which you feel unsure how to pray. One mother shared a recent conversation with her daughter-in-law-to-be. The young woman announced that once they wed, every Thanksgiving and Christmas would be spent with her family. This mother could not even think of a response. Perhaps the young woman's mother will speak on behalf of the young man's family to her daughter, but in the meantime, the son's parents feel devastated.

"Likewise the Spirit helps us in our weakness; for we do not know how to pray as we ought, but the Spirit himself intercedes for us, with sighs too deep for words" (Romans 8:26).

Another mother wrote, "I feel as if I have been banished into time-out exile, shunned by silence." With time to recollect, she wrote about a word picture that came to her in prayer. "They have closed the door to their own room, but I dwell in a spacious house. I am free to walk about and serve and to hope for all of our sakes that they will open the door. Jesus can walk through the door closed to me, and I ask him to go where I cannot." Later she wrote that they had reconciled.

We must guard our hearts. If we do not find our peace in the Lord, we can become bitter or resentful. With Jesus, reconciliation and healing can happen.

I think some mothers- and daughters-in-law have such high expectations for a close relationship that when, for whatever reason, it is not, they can feel very disappointed. One woman shared how much she had hoped her mother-in-law would be another mother for her. She had wanted someone who noticed the great job she did, gave her words of affirmation, and was interested in her life. Instead, when they were together she felt like an outsider; she could not get into the woman's heart.

Her mother-in-law probably did not realize that her lack of affirmation communicated that she did not want a close relationship. Perhaps she was not even capable of opening up like that. Maybe the daughter-in-law's expectations were unrealistic.

For mothers-in-law who feel as if they want to open up to a daughter-in-law but do not know how, I encourage you to make a gesture. Start small: Invite her to lunch or coffee sometime. It is not too late until one of you is dead! Just an invitation may open one heart to the other.

Sometimes a mother-in-law is unsure she is significant enough to her daughter-in-law for the young woman to care about time with her or compliments from her. If that is your situation, take the risk and believe your daughter-in-law wants a good relationship, just as your daughters do.

One new mother-in-law wrote to me about the intensity of her pain in the midst of difficulty. "I vacillate between offering up the suffering of the wave of pain that is grieflike and then feeling exhilarated by the joy of relinquishment to God's will. I feel stricken and afflicted. I feel used and judged, cast aside like something that is no longer needed." Later she experienced deep restoration in the relationship.

These difficult moments may be the birth pains of very deep love. If you offer them in union with the cross, they are not wasted suffering. If you are either a daughter- or mother-in-law experiencing difficulty, the way of the cross is important. Accept unjust suffering, embrace the cross as Christ did, including being misunderstood. He prayed from the cross, "Father, forgive them; for they know not what they do" (Luke 23:34). He is your example. Pray to forgive your in-laws for ways they do not know they are hurting you. Like Mary, seek to be an advocate rather than an accuser.

Unintended pain from a child happens. I found in my journal the following entry about one of our teens: "My child cared not when I was in agony in pregnancy, in labor, preparing for a C-section, hemorrhaging postpartum, exhausted from sleepless nights, or hurting with infections. For years a child gives little thought to the pain he causes a parent, because his own pain is ever before him. I do the same thing, ignoring ways my sins have caused Jesus pain, shame, and agony while focusing on my discomfort."

We complicate our sufferings through our flaws, failures, and sins. Remember the analogy of digging a deeper well? God can use our difficult circumstances to deepen our love for any child and any in-law, so that we become a deeper reservoir of grace for our family. Thank God, his grace is abundant and available for us all!

BLESSED PARENTS-IN-LAW

Following the deaths of her husband and two sons in a foreign land, Naomi decided to return home to Bethlehem. She released her daughters-in-law to return to their families, but Ruth clung to her, choosing her as her spiritual mother. Ruth went with Naomi back to Israel and followed Naomi's advice.

Through Naomi's guidance, Ruth married Boaz and had a beautiful son named Obed. The women of Bethlehem told Naomi, "He shall be to you a restorer of life and a nourisher of your old age; for your daughter-in-law who loves you, who is more to you than seven sons, has borne him" (Ruth 4:15).

What a beautiful comment! Naomi and Ruth's special relationship was a witness to the townspeople.

When Moses was forty, he was banished from Egypt. In the desert he met his wife among the Midianites. Forty years later Moses led the people of Israel out of Egypt. When his father-in-law, Jethro, came to see how Moses was managing, he saw Moses' utter exhaustion. He advised him with wisdom. "So Moses gave heed to the voice of his father-in-law and did all that he had said" (Exodus 18:24). Moses did not owe Jethro obedience, but he honored his wise father-in-law and trusted his advice.

We lead with love, not criticism. We need to be more interested in understanding our in-laws than in being understood. We speak all of the love languages to them, as we do our children. When we discover their primary love language, we speak that one more directly, so they feel the love we have for them.

We pray to build bridges with our in-laws rather than barriers. At the same time we maintain boundaries that enable our family of families to flourish. We pray for wisdom, insight, and understanding. We claim the promise found in Romans 8:28, "We know that in everything God works for good with those who love him, who are called according to his purpose." God is at work in all of us.

CHAPTER TWELVE

Consolidating Our Gains as a Growing Family

MARRIAGE IS A MISSION

In *The Mystery of Marriage,* Mike Mason issues the following challenge:

> Holy matrimony, like other holy orders, was never intended as a comfort station for lazy people. On the contrary, it is a systematic program of deliberate and thoroughgoing self-sacrifice.... Marriage is really a drastic course of action.... It is a radical step and is not intended for anyone who is not prepared, indeed eager, to surrender his own will and to be wholeheartedly submissive to the will of another.[1]

Marriage is not for the faint of heart!

How can we support young couples in their first year of marriage? Often problems do not emerge until a couple is actually married. One spouse might want counseling, but the other may feel that counseling is only for marriages in serious trouble.

What if the priest who married the couple scheduled two "wellness checkups" during their first year of marriage? Pastors could not withhold the sacrament to force compliance, but most couples seeking marriage in the Church want their marriage to flourish. If the appointments were set, they would have a ready opportunity to get help so as to avoid serious difficulties later.

The parish could also acknowledge couples celebrating their one-year anniversary. Each couple would experience the support and encouragement of their pastor *and* the parish. They would know they were not on their own.

We want marriages to witness to the world about Christ's living presence and to reflect his relationship to the Church "by the mutual love of the spouses, by their generous fruitfulness, their solidarity and faithfulness, and by the loving way in which all members of the family work together."[2]

How do we undergird, rather than undermine, the marriages in our extended family? We strengthen young couples' marriages with our love, our time, our wisdom (when we are asked), and our money (when we are able).

MENTORING YOUNG MOTHERS

Scripture calls older women, in particular, to mentor. "So train the young women to love their husbands and children, to be sensible, chaste, domestic, kind and submissive to their husbands, that the word of God may not be discredited" (Titus 2:4–5). Those of us who are older have a task we simply cannot delegate—God's Word is on the line. We should be available to mentor the younger women; younger women should be open to being mentored.

Advice for the bride. My mom shared a few thoughts at a bridal shower for my first daughter-in-law, Sarah: Go to bed together and rise together as much as possible; a united life should be the norm. Choose what you will have for dinner when you finish your breakfast. Set the table before you begin dinner, and have dinner ready on time.

Since my marriage, I have been very blessed by ways my mom and mother-in-law have cared for me, woman to woman. Though we have never lived close, they have anticipated my needs, offered me hope, cared for me, and prayed for me. They have invited me out, cooked for me, visited me in the hospital, and given me clothes. God has also brought other women into my life who have mothered me.

MOTHERING THE MOTHER

Mentors of young moms are comparable to shepherds who gently lead those who are with young (see Isaiah 40:11). What are some of the needs of young mothers? How can we offer personal care for them?

Pregnancy. Do not wait for the baby's arrival before you offer help. Though we cannot stay with the couple for three months, as Mary did with Elizabeth, we can meet some of the mother's needs before the baby arrives. What about maternity clothes that make her feel beautiful, including a maternity swimsuit? It is fun to send something new, even in the last couple months of pregnancy. Does she have good nursing bras? Usually the eighth month is a good time to buy them. Could you send a gift card for a last dinner date before life changes?

Post-delivery. I have promised each of my sons and their wives that, if they want, I will come for a full week every time they have a baby. (This is what my mom did for me.) Scott understands that means sacrifices for him at home (as did my dad), but he also understands the value of the help.

I think most women prefer their own moms to visit first, so I make my plans with the couple once they know when my daughter-in-law's mom will come. What a privilege for me to serve each family in this way. I begin to "know" this new little person and savor the moments together. I run errands, cook, clean, do laundry, or pack if they are moving. If they already have a child, I get extra special time with that little one.

If the young mom is recovering from a C-section, she will have limitations on driving and picking up anything (or anyone) heavier than the newborn. Are there errands to be done? Does she need a ride to her or the baby's doctor's office? Is there vacuuming or any other housework that involves stretching, bending, or kneeling?

Nursing. Nursing is a beautiful way to nurture a baby and to help mom recover. It helps her stop bleeding and releases mothering hormones. She should build up nursing time slowly—three minutes per side, then four, five, and so on. (I assumed with my sixth child that I did not need to build up the time—and I was wrong! I got very painful cracked and bleeding nipples.)

A large diaper pin fastened to the bra on the side last nursed reminds a mom which side she should nurse next. If she lets one breast air-dry while nursing with the other, keeping a pad under it to catch any extra milk, she will limit chafing. Though her baby gets less air with nursing than with bottle-feeding, she will want to burp after nursing each side. She will probably find a rocking chair with extra pillows for support very helpful.

A nice gift is a pretty nursing nightgown and robe or pajamas. Another idea is a water bottle, to help remind the mom to drink a lot of water when she is nursing. I like to give men's

100-percent cotton handkerchiefs as nursing pads. The all-natural fiber is gentle on skin. The handkerchiefs are inexpensive and washable, and their many layers hold a lot of milk. Another great gift is a large supply of diapers or a few weeks of diaper service.

WOMAN-TO-WOMAN WISDOM

Adult companionship. Being alone most of the day can make a woman feel isolated. Can you call? Can you visit and offer to take her out to lunch? Check with her first about the best time, since a baby's missed naptime can add stress.

One-on-one time with her husband. If you live close, can you babysit for them? If not, can they swap sit with another couple, so each gets a date every other Friday night? Or can you send them babysitting money or a restaurant gift card?

Funds. Can you offer coupons or send care packages? Can you give gifts that relieve some of the pressure? (More on this later.)

Support and practical help. Can you schedule a visit, and not just when there is a new baby in the house? Can you take the baby on a walk or to the park so Mom can nap? Sometimes young moms feel better after cutting down excessive noise, exercising, or finishing a book or project. After a rough night, encourage her to take it easy.

Assisting young mothers is pro-life work. Practical help, plus your prayers, may help prevent mommy burnout and even open the couple's hearts to another child.

Domestic skills. Tread carefully; never criticize. If you find a good book on homemaking, pass it along. I suggest resources in *Graced and Gifted.*[3]

Young moms who have domestic skills may be frustrated by their own perfectionism. Help them live with imperfection as they move toward greater order. Perhaps dads can share some cleaning responsibilities until moms are fully recovered from delivery.

A sense of accomplishment. Someone called me on a day I was frustrated with doing "nothing." Michael was three months old. My friend asked me if I had fed, diapered, and dressed him and made my bed. When I said yes, she responded, "You have done so much! And are you working on dinner?" I smiled. She let me know that, at that stage in life, I was doing a lot. Those few words of encouragement meant so much.

Timing is everything when it comes to a young mother renewing her hobbies, interests, skills, gifts, and passions. There will be a season when these fit her family's life, though perhaps not for a while. A small outlet might be possible with your help or the help of her husband or a friend.

Reasonable goals. Too much idealism or a difficult baby can leave a young mom feeling disillusioned. Since children thrive on routine, they may eventually set a schedule that the mom can keep. Can you let her vent in the meantime? Assure her that you do not think less of her as a woman of God because she is down, upset, or having a lousy day or a few lousy nights.

Rewards. When my sister-in-law Amy told me she was having her sixth baby, I said, "I wish I could put on a parade for you! You are such an awesome mother. Thank you for blessing us with all of these little nieces and nephews."

Go ahead and praise that young mom. Let her know you appreciate her. Express your thanks to her on Mother's Day and to her husband on Father's Day, recognizing their many sacrifices for their little ones.

Confidence. Your "attaboys" at the right time, coupled with advice when asked, help a mom grow in confidence. Assure her of her motherly instincts. Remind her that you are only a call away. Encourage her to glean what she can from "experts" but then do what is on her heart. (Even experts can offer conflicting advice.) Send her a note after you see how well she is doing, or send e-mails or letters affirming her vision for caring for her husband and children, with special quotes from saints or Church documents.

Time for prayer. If you live close by, can you watch the baby so she can attend Mass alone or have a holy hour? Encourage her to offer her ordinary work as part of her prayer, so she can release extraordinary grace through mundane chores. Tell her about upcoming retreats so she can plan for babysitters. Perhaps you could fund the retreat or help coordinate sitting for several young moms whose husbands are unavailable.

Preparing for a move. Encourage young moms not to cluster major life changes, though some may not have an option about having a baby and moving for a new job. Order in a mom's schedule helps even when there is little order in the home due to packing or unpacking. Can she plan some meals out or accept friends' offers to bring over meals? If she switches to paper plates and cups the last couple of days, she can pack the kitchen sooner. Encourage her to pray for her spouse as he also deals with the changes and challenges of the move and a new job.

A sense of humor. We need to keep a light heart. I wrote these thoughts while I had several small children. You know you are a mother of young children when…

- You tie your own shoes in knots.
- You leave a gathering of adults waving and saying, "Bye-bye!"
- You cannot go three days without a nap.
- You say, "I have to go potty."
- You can lift two children and three bags while unlocking the car door.

Share humorous stories with a young mom, and enjoy her stories.

MOTHERING THE FATHER

Whatever we do for a young dad, we want to strengthen and not subvert his critical role. He is the primary ally, guide, and coach for his beloved. When the couple conceives a child, the dad's relationship to the child is mediated by his wife. Until delivery he does not feel the same connection that she does, but as he loves his wife, he nurtures his baby.

His concerns will probably center on how he will provide for this child and how he can best support his wife as she transitions to the role of mother. Encourage him in his prayer life, since the Lord is the source of all that he needs to be a good husband and father. (This is especially good coming from his father or father-in-law.)

Offer practical help. A baby shower affirms the joy of bringing new life into the world and surrounds the couple with caring family and friends. Practically they acquire baby clothing and equipment they need, an added blessing for the father who is concerned about providing for the baby. Often grandparents purchase one of the larger pieces of baby equipment.

When Michael and Ana shared with fellow grad students at Notre Dame that they had conceived on their honeymoon, one student teased, "NFP doesn't work, does it?"

Michael responded, "NFP? We weren't using NFP. I knew God was calling me to be a husband. I hoped he was calling me to be a father. If he wants me to be a scholar, he'll confirm that." Their example has encouraged other grad students to weigh their reasons for delaying being open to new life.

Before Sarah delivered their firstborn, I wrote to Gabriel, "Jesus is the source of love from which you will draw all you need to give yourself in sacrificial love to your spouse. Though you do not have a direct role to play in nurturing this life yet, your love for Sarah, celebrating her motherhood, is the way you love your baby best. Keep Christ at the center: He is the model for love's radical demands."

Gabriel's presence to assist Sarah, and Michael's to support Ana, contributed to the peaceful deliveries of their babies and their shared joy.

Money

It is a joy for parents to share financial resources with their children, even when they are financially independent. Caution: If parents habitually bail out children when they are irresponsible, the young adults will not learn lessons they need to learn. For instance, if parents cosign a loan for money the young adults will not have, those parents are digging a ditch of debt that will hinder, not help, their children. In turn, this sets the stage for stress in the relationship.

On the other hand, if parents observe the young adults managing their money with maturity, then parents can be generous. Their generosity will strengthen and not weaken their children. Some parents work so hard to provide an inheritance for their children that they miss the critical years they could provide significant help.

Ask your son or son-in-law if a financial gift would be welcome. We do not want a gift to be construed as a judgment that he is not providing well. We must not offer a gift in a way that makes the couple feel like dependent children. The goal of a gift is to strengthen them. They can politely refuse our gift without any hurt feelings, or they can accept our gift with no strings attached.

Never slip your married son or daughter some money; that is deceptive. It would definitely undercut his or her marriage. Ask what the couple's needs are, and help if you can. It is a blessing to have the children, including the in-laws, make a Christmas wish list, so we can shop for items they most want and need.

I enjoy imitating a tradition my mother had with us. Just before Advent I prepare a package for each couple, containing a few new decorations, a wreath, cookie cutters, or towels, plus a set of Advent candles (hard to find, especially with one or more babies in tow). These are items that are rarely in the young couple's budget, and the wife appreciates being able to prepare her home for Advent and then Christmas.

One Thanksgiving Gabriel and Sarah had settled the baby for a nap, and I offered, "Here's ten bucks. Why don't you grab an afternoon ice cream date? I promise I'll call on the cell phone if Veronica wakes up."

They were thrilled, and so was I! Two hours later when they returned, Veronica was still asleep. It was such a joy to be available and helpful.

GRANDPARENTING

"Grandchildren are the crown of the aged" (Proverbs 17:6). We do not deserve grandchildren; they are pure gift. Think about it: no pregnancy, no morning sickness or stretch marks or weight gain, no delivery or recovery. Yet our children place these little ones in our arms and say they are ours! There is no blessing like it; it is truly an experience of grace. Who in their right mind could be negative about a grandchild?

God is faithful to us, and he calls us to be faithful to him. The Lord redeems individuals, but I believe he loves to save whole families. So we proclaim his faithfulness to future generations. "For the LORD is good; his mercy endures forever, and his faithfulness to all generations" (Psalm 100:5).

It is not merely a good idea for us to share the faith with the next generation; it is a command. "My spirit which is upon you, and my words which I have put in your mouth, shall not depart out of your mouth, or out of the mouth of your children, or out of the mouth of your children's children, says the LORD, from this time forth and for evermore" (Isaiah 59:21).

How can you evangelize your great-grandchildren (and beyond)? Record your life of faith, or use the St. Joseph Communcations' Legacy of Faith and Devotion program to preserve your faith journey for future generations.[4]

We bless future generations through our faithfulness. "But the mercy of the LORD is from everlasting to everlasting upon those who fear him, and his righteousness to children's children, to those who keep his covenant and remember to do his commandments" (Psalm 103:17–18). Each one of us becomes a channel of grace to the others.

In 2008 Pope Benedict XVI wrote this beautiful Universal Prayer for the Catholic Grandparents' Association:

> Lord Jesus,
> you were born of the Virgin Mary,
> the daughter of Saints Joachim and Anne.
> Look with love on grandparents the world over.
> Protect them! They are a source of enrichment
> for families, for the Church and for all of society.
> Support them! As they grow older,
> may they continue to be for their families
> strong pillars of Gospel faith,
> guardians of noble domestic ideals,
> living treasuries of sound religious traditions.
> Make them teachers of wisdom and courage,
> that they may pass on to future generations the fruits
> of their mature human and spiritual experience.
>
> Lord Jesus,
> help families and society
> to value the presence and role of grandparents.
> May they never be ignored or excluded,
> but always encounter respect and love.
> Help them to live serenely and to feel welcomed
> in all the years of life which you give them.

Mary, Mother of all the living,
keep grandparents constantly in your care,
accompany them on their earthly pilgrimage,
and by your prayers, grant that all families
may one day be reunited in our heavenly homeland,
where you await all humanity
for the great embrace of life without end. Amen![5]

God bless each one of you who are in this phase of life. The Lord has great things in store for your extended family as you bridge the gap between those who have gone before you and those who are coming after you.

PART SIX

A Woman Who Fears the Lord

Is to Be Praised

—Proverbs 31:30

CHAPTER THIRTEEN

Witness to the World

Look briefly at the "Priority Living" illustration in this book's introduction. Notice the horizontal circles around the core relationships. These circles represent your priorities that are not essential to your core relationships but that are very important—the periphery. Your periphery includes your extended family, your parish, your community, your country, and the world.

BALANCING PRIORITIES

The Proverbs 31 woman is praised for keeping her priorities straight. "Many women have done excellently, but you surpass them all" (Proverbs 31:29). What has she done well? She is "a woman who fears the Lord" (Proverbs 31:30). She has honored the Lord with her love for him, especially through her vocation as a wife and mother. She has shown love for her neighbors. She has lived the truth expressed by St. Paul, "Owe no one anything, except to love one another; for he who loves his neighbor has fulfilled the law" (Romans 13:8).

The world within is her vocation—her family. But there is a world outside of her family, her periphery, that is also a priority in her faith.

We follow the example of the Proverbs 31 woman. We cannot neglect our family to serve others; service has to fit our phase in life. But we should do whatever good we can. And we anticipate a time in life when we will have more time, energy, and finances to offer.

Where in our priorities do we place extended family relationships? Do we actually insert them ahead of where they should be? Or do we neglect them? Where do neighbors and the quality of life in our neighborhood fit? What is our civic duty toward our town or city, state, and country?

Beyond that, do we care about the millions of people who do not know Jesus? How do we develop a sense of mission-mindedness in our children?

We must avoid two extremes: focusing so much on our families that we altogether neglect other priorities, *and* allowing lesser priorities to dominate. Since balance is our goal, let's discuss where the peripheral priorities fit into our lives.

A person's final words are very significant as a statement of priorities. Acts 1:8 and Matthew 28:18–20 record Jesus' final words to his beloved apostles, just before he ascended to the Father. Jesus declared his plan for evangelizing the world: "But you shall receive power when the Holy Spirit has come upon you; and you shall be my witnesses in Jerusalem and in all Judea and Samaria and to the end of the earth" (Acts 1:8). The disciples were to begin in Jerusalem and expand to the outlying area of Judea. Then they would continue into the neighboring country of Samaria and beyond to the entire world.

These concentric circles of priority are also our periphery. We'll look at two of them in this chapter and two in the next.

PERIPHERY RING #1—JERUSALEM:
THOSE CLOSEST TO US

Our extended family. Our marriage is a part of a larger family of families. How do we as a couple prioritize the time and money necessary to maintain strong relationships within the extended family? How often should we get together? If money is limited, are there other ways we can communicate our love besides gifts and travel? How frequently do we write or call to keep lines of communication open?

Extended family can be one of the toughest places for us to live our faith well. Mary is our model. First, she brings Jesus to Elizabeth. Then she stays and serves Elizabeth for three months. Like Mary, we want to bring Christ to our relatives as well as serve them in practical ways.

In his *Letter to Families*, Blessed Pope John Paul II said, "Who is more of a neighbor than one's own family members, parents and children?"[1] We must not overlook extended family as part of our mission field. We need to care enough for their souls to share the faith while we care for their needs. We share the truth *and* live it in a vibrant, joyful way.

Dear friends. We have friends who sometimes fill the gaps when family is not close. This is God's provision for our needs. "Your friend and your father's friend, do not forsake; and do not go to your brother's house in the day of your calamity. Better is a neighbor who is near than a brother who is far away" (Proverbs 27:10).

Godchildren. Often parents honor their relatives and close friends by choosing them as godparents for their children. "The best place...to look [is among] relatives, even grandparents, who have a blood relationship with the godchild and have kept the faith over the years. Good friends are also appropriate, but sometimes friendships wane, leaving the godchild without an active godparent."[2]

Godparents represent the Church to the baptized child. At least one godparent has to be a Catholic in good standing who has received the sacraments of Baptism, Holy Communion, and Confirmation, which may include older siblings. If there are two godparents, they must be of opposite sexes. After the parents, the godparents are the ones responsible for the child's spiritual formation.[3] If a godparent is not fulfilling his own obligations to live the faith, how can he assist the child?

If you are a godparent, what can you do for your godchild? You can pray daily for this child and act on inspirations you receive. You can remind the child of your prayer for him or her and ask for specific prayer requests. If the child lives close by, you can invite him over for a meal or offer to take her out.

Godparents can give gifts—something fun as well as something spiritual. They can attend their godchild's reception of other sacraments. And they can correspond or call to keep in touch, so that the love of Christ is at the heart of the relationship.

The household of faith in our local parish. I was driving up Sunset Boulevard and noticed a newly demolished car dealership. "David, isn't this exciting?" I asked my eight-year-old. "They've taken down this building so they can build something!"

David responded, "It's very sad."

"Sad?" I never imagined this would be his response.

"My children will never know the town of my youth."

"The town of your youth," I replied, "is still being built!"

In a way David captured a sentiment you may have regarding the Church. Let me assure you, however, that the Church of your youth is still being built! The Church is still on the move; God is fulfilling his plan. We are a part of this: We have a part to play in history and in salvation history. This is an exciting time in which to live. *This* is our opportunity to become saints!

As parts of the body of Christ, we have unique gifts and abilities from the Holy Spirit to serve the Church, especially in our local parish (see Romans 12:4–8; 1 Corinthians 12; Ephesians 4:11–16). This is not a matter of pride in our giftedness but of humility in service. We are to be doers—not only hearers—of the Word, which includes living our vocation to love as part of the Church militant on Earth. So we ask the Lord, In what ways should I serve?

We have stages of life when we can be more or less involved in our parish or community. Where does using our gifts and talents, expressed in apostolate, fit our priorities? If we think of our talents as an expression of who we are in Christ (our person), then we place apostolate as a higher priority than even our marriage (our partner). However, apostolate (periphery) is really a lesser priority than our marriage. When we place our priorities properly, even our work in apostolate strengthens our marriage and family life, and vice versa.

We need to cultivate an interior, private faith life as well as an external, public expression of that faith. (Some people's faith is so private, *they* are not even sure it exists.) We witness publicly in our parish. "I have not hidden your saving help within my heart, I have spoken of your faithfulness and your salvation; I have not concealed your mercy and your faithfulness from the great congregation" (Psalm 40:10).

The pastor is not the only person who should make an effort in the parish. I once heard this definition of a football game: twenty-two people in desperate need of a rest; thousands in desperate need of exercise. A parish can be described as a pastor and a handful of parishioners who are in desperate need of rest. Everyone else is on the sidelines, in desperate need of spiritual exercise.

THE EARLY CHURCH: A MODEL FOR OUR PARISH

As the lay faithful we are called "to take an active, conscientious, and responsible part in the mission of the Church *in this great moment in history*."[4] We participate in the mission of our local parish first. In our parish we can imitate the four ways the early Church was strengthened: "And they held steadfastly to the apostles' teaching and fellowship, to the breaking of the bread and to the prayers" (Acts 2:42).

The apostles' teaching. We begin with adult faith formation, for the parish "is a privileged place for the catechesis of children *and parents*" (*CCC*, 2226, emphasis added). Catechesis is not supposed to stop after confirmation. "Religious education and the catechesis of children make the family a true *subject of evangelization and the apostolate* within the Church."[5] We should keep learning the faith, especially so that we can teach our children well.

More adult faith formation is happening in Catholic parishes than ever before. All adults should have a Bible and the *Catechism*, so they can read and understand the apostles' teaching. Through the St. Paul Center for Biblical Theology, Scott and I and others have developed introductory-level Scripture studies. We train laypeople so they can offer these six- to seven-week studies in their parishes.[6]

You could share this *Life-Nurturing Love* series with parishioners—even just a few—in your home or parish center. Other excellent Scripture studies include Jeff Cavins's *The Great Adventure* and *Catholic Scripture Studies*. I also recommend Bible studies by Stacy Mitch, Michaelann Martin, Curtis Martin, Tim Gray, and Ted Sri, published through Emmaus Road Publishing.[7] These resources will assist you in understanding Sacred Scripture in new ways.

Lighthouse Catholic Media/NFP kiosks are in hundreds of American parishes.[8] For a three-dollar donation, you can purchase CDs of various Catholic teachers. If you have a long commute or vacation, this could be a great way for you and your family to learn your faith better. (If we listen to the talks in the car, we call it "car-techesis.")

Fellowship. The second area for strengthening parish life is fellowship—a caring community that connects families and single people as the family of God. This is much more than a social time over coffee and donuts, though social interaction contributes to a sense of community. Fellowship expresses our communion as God's people, united to each other as members of the body of Christ. Blessed Pope John Paul II urged, "It is important that families attempt to build bonds of solidarity among themselves. This allows them to assist each other in the educational enterprise: parents are educated by other parents, and children by other children."[9]

We share our treasure by tithing, at least in part, to our local parish. We financially support our parish works of mercy and call others to contribute as well.

We share our time. As St. Josemaría Escrivá says, we have "an obligation to do apostolate."[10] We can participate in preparation classes for marriage or the Rite of Christian Initiation of Adults. We can chaperone youth retreats or youth mission trips. We can visit parishioners who are ill or homebound. We can reach out to those in prison on behalf of our parish. We can cook or serve meals for the bereaved following a funeral Mass. And we can assist in parish pro-life efforts, like the Life Chain, 40 Days for Life, and the March for Life in Washington on January 22 each year.

We share our talents. We strengthen our parish when we organize or teach in children's catechetical programs or volunteer with the youth group. We assist at Mass as lectors, eucharistic ministers, or in music ministry.

If there is a place for everyone in the parish, where does a contemplative person fit? He may not want to have a public role, but he could enlist a family to pray a novena for a particular intention of the parish. Or perhaps he could sign up for a holy hour or help organize eucharistic adoration at the parish.

Women have unique opportunities for developing apostolate, woman to woman, at the parish level. We can offer each other words of wisdom and prayer. We can encourage friends to join us at a women's conference and then return home refreshed, ready to reach out to others. We can lead Bible studies in our homes, like the *Life-Nurturing Love* series. We can network, offering each other practical help, like the Sisters of Ruth in Steubenville, Ohio (moms helping moms with meals or rides), or the Franciscan University Ministry to Moms program (college women who donate time to area families on a weekly basis).

We encourage young parents that caring for their children is a genuine apostolate. They can pray together for their parish and pastor, as well as missionaries from their parish. They can pray by name for those preparing for the diaconate and the priesthood in the diocese. (We keep our seminarians' photos on our fridge.) They can plant the seeds for apostolates in their children's hearts and look for ways they can reach out to others as a family. And they can anticipate a time for great parish involvement as fits their life circumstances.

Breaking of the bread. The third way the early Church was strengthened was through the breaking of the bread, the Eucharist. We renew our spiritual life and our parish by participating in the eucharistic life of our parish community.

Do we know which parishioners have stopped coming to Mass and why? Some people are unable to come due to an infirmity or illness. Could we become a eucharistic minister and then bring our Lord to the homebound or those in the hospital?

Sometimes people do not come to Mass because they feel as if nobody notices whether or not they are there. Perhaps we need to extend a personal invitation. Catholics Come Home has produced beautiful ads, broadcast nationally, to make it easier for us to invite people to come home to the Church.[11]

Prayer. The early Church was strengthened through prayer; so are we. Prayer is the soul of any apostolate. Do we spend more time talking *about* God than *to* him? If Jesus needed time alone for prayer (see Matthew 14:23; Luke 4:42), we know we do.

We need to undergird apostolate with prayer. We pray for the priests, religious, and missionaries who serve us. Then we ask them, what are your needs? How can we help you?

PERIPHERY RING #2—JUDEA:
CARE FOR NEIGHBORS

"Neighbors" are actual neighbors. Jesus illustrated how to love neighbors through the parable of the Good Samaritan: Neighbors are people in need. However, we may be so quick to think of this that we neglect our actual neighbors.

This is one of the few weaknesses in my upbringing: We did not know our neighbors. Between church and school commitments, we did not have much time to meet them. We did not even know most of their names. Now I have lived in the same neighborhood for more than twenty years. I know many of my neighbors but not all. Last summer a neighbor across the street died in her home, and it was two days before anyone knew she was gone. That is so sad.

Can we introduce ourselves to neighbors, as they work in their yards or walk by ours with a child or a pet? Can other neighbors introduce us to each other?

When we were new to the area, our little boys were playing baseball in our front yard one morning with some neighbor boys they had just met. I had not noticed the time; they had been up since 7:00 AM, and the game did not start before 8:30. When a neighbor threw open the sash and shouted, "Hey, some of us work all week!" I realized I had offended my neighbor. My introduction to him was an apology.

We should be thoughtful neighbors, taking care of our yard and home, collecting trash, and parking in a way that does not inconvenience others. We can be sensitive to our neighbors' concerns without being controlled by them. We can participate in neighborhood gatherings, such as Fourth of July parades, backyard barbecues, or a rosary walk around the block. We can help plan a block party. This is a part of our witness before we open our mouths to share the gospel.

How can we share our faith? When we lived in Milwaukee, I participated in Christmas teas. Women would invite neighbors for cookies and tea, and I would share the gospel. I was able to build on already established friendships, and the women could follow up later.

When we lived in Joliet, Illinois, on Easter weekend I walked up and down the street with my three little children. We gave each family a white carnation with a small message about the importance of Easter. I had only met two of my neighbors, though we had lived there for eight months. Rather than wait until someone reached out to me, I decided to extend friendship.

Here in Steubenville, Ohio, we enjoy caroling with friends around our neighborhood, proclaiming the Good News in a nonthreatening way. Twice a year neighbors collect trash strewn about the neighborhood. Sometimes neighbors assist each other by caring for someone's yard or painting their home.

My friend Suzy, who calls herself "just an ordinary Catholic," moved with her family to a cul-de-sac in southern California. She introduced herself to her neighbors and discovered that many had been raised Catholic but for various reasons were not practicing the faith.

Suzy has a winsome way. She would say, "Oh, you weren't married in the Church? Our priest would be happy to bless your marriage. We have Pre-Cana classes. I'll get you the information." "You've been baptized but never confirmed? Come to our Confirmation classes." "You've been baptized, but your children have not? Let me introduce you to our parish priest, and he can help you get them baptized."

In just two years many of the families began attending Mass again. In one home the wife was confirmed, two children were baptized, and the husband received First Communion and Confirmation. In a second, two children received First Communion. In a third, two children received First Communion, and their parents' marriage was blessed. In a fourth, an adult was baptized and received her First Communion, and her two children were baptized.

That was the fruit of Suzy's neighborliness, coupled with fun get-togethers. She lived her faith so vibrantly that many lives were changed. Her motivation should be ours: Let's bring as many people to heaven with us as possible.

Sometimes neighbors need someone to listen to their difficulties rather than solve their problems. A four-year-old had a neighbor who had just lost his wife. The child noticed the man sitting on his front porch, crying. The little boy went over and crawled up on his lap.

When he returned home, his mother asked, "What did you say to him?"

"Nothing," he replied. "I just helped him cry."

There are practical things you can do. If there are elderly people who live near you, you can shovel their driveway or walkway, rake their leaves, or put their trashcans away. You might even pair up families in the neighborhood: those without older relatives nearby with older people who do not have children or grandchildren in town.

You can take a meal to someone who just had a baby or to a family in crisis. If new people move into the neighborhood, you can drop off a meal, including paper plates, cups, and napkins so they can unpack after dinner instead of doing dishes. You can also give them your phone number in case they need something like tools or trash bags.

In 1999 we had a murder in our neighborhood. Some of the families decided they needed to take back the neighborhood, in a sense. They began a rosary walk, which is still held every Friday evening during the summer months. Babies in strollers, people with canes, families, single people, priests, and seminarians gather at the home of some Marian priests and walk a large block, praying the rosary and singing the Divine Mercy Chaplet. It takes about forty-five minutes. People watch from their porches; others join. It is a powerful way of saying, "Satan, you don't own this neighborhood."

You cannot force friendship, but you can offer it. "As much as you can, aim to know your neighbors, and consult with the wise" (Sirach 9:14).

You do not always have to answer the probing questions of a neighbor. "If you have understanding, answer your neighbor; but if not, put your hand on your mouth" (Sirach 5:12). For reasons of protecting the privacy of another or even keeping someone safe, we may need to keep silent.

Avoid gossip about neighbors. "He who belittles his neighbor lacks sense, but a man of understanding remains silent. He who goes about as a tale bearer reveals secrets, but he who is trustworthy in spirit keeps a thing hidden" (Proverbs 11:12–13).

Give neighbors the benefit of the doubt, extending trust. "Judge your neighbor's feelings by your own, and in every matter be thoughtful" (Sirach 31:15).

At the same time, allow personal space with neighbors. "Let your foot be seldom in your neighbor's house, lest he become weary of you and hate you" (Proverbs 25:17). Visit neighbors, but do not overdo it.

"Neighbor" according to the Good Samaritan parable. Jesus made it clear that our "neighbor" includes someone we see in spiritual or physical need. Blessed Pope John Paul II said, "The faith-filled witness of Christian families is an essential element in the new evangelization to which the Holy Spirit is calling the Church in our time."[12] Both our individual witness and the witness of our families include sharing the Christian faith *and* addressing the needs around us.

We should share our faith in conjunction with compassionately meeting needs; otherwise our actions are simply social works without context. At the same time we have to do good works that authenticate our faith. "What does it profit, my brethren, if a man says he has faith but has not works? Can his faith save him?... So faith by itself, if it has no works, is dead" (James 2:14, 17). We meet the needs of those around us while we share the good news of Jesus Christ, so that their deepest needs will also be met.

CHAPTER FOURTEEN

This Is Our Time

How does our faith make a difference in our country and our world, as we continue the theme from Acts 1:8? How do we apply the lordship of Jesus Christ in our culture? And how do we proclaim his salvation throughout the world?

PERIPHERY RING #3—SAMARIA: OUR CULTURE

Jesus is the source of all truth, justice, and lasting peace. The more we understand the principles of a just society, the more we can know our role in fleshing out those principles in our laws. All law expresses morality; the only question is, whose?

St. Paul was keenly aware of his place as a Christian and a Roman citizen when he wrote, "Let every person be subject to the governing authorities. For there is no authority except from God, and those that exist have been instituted by God" (Romans 13:1). No matter how secular a society, public authorities only have power according to God's plan. They are public servants for whom we should pray regularly.

"When the righteous are in authority, the people rejoice; but when the wicked rule, the people groan" (Proverbs 29:2). If we have leaders who are not godly, we pray for their salvation and for the grace to bear the hardships we face from their leadership. Then we work to get better leaders elected.

As Christians we engage our society rather than withdraw from it, sharing the wisdom of God for the good of all. "But the wisdom from above is first pure, then peaceable, gentle, open to reason, full of mercy and good fruits, without uncertainty or insincerity. And the harvest of righteousness is sown in peace by those who make peace" (James 3:17–18).

Yes, we pray. We also use our freedoms to proclaim the gospel *and* to speak for the rights of individuals and families, especially those who cannot speak for themselves.

The genius of women. Blessed Pope John Paul II taught that women have important contributions to make in both society and the Church. "It is thus my hope, dear sisters, that you will reflect carefully on what it means to speak of the '*genius of women*'...in order to let this genius be more fully expressed in the life of society as a whole, as well as in the life of the Church."[1]

The genius of women is rooted in our natural tendency to see persons more than tasks. This is a gentling force that our culture needs, though our involvement publicly will depend on our stage in life.

My paternal grandmother, Gladys Kirk, was a homemaker and an excellent example of a woman who served her community as a volunteer in many organizations. My grandfather had represented King County for three terms as a Washington state representative before he took a position in the Treasury Department. Then my grandmother was elected to his former seat and served seven consecutive terms with grace and dignity and without a feminist ax to grind. She accomplished much for the people of her district and state and was greatly respected by the assembly.

As an honorary page at age twelve, I saw my grandmother in action in committee work and on the floor of the

Washington State House. I am so grateful for the heritage she and my grandfather gave me in public service for God and country.

The principle of subsidiarity. Families are sovereign societies within societies. In his *Letter to Families*, Blessed Pope John Paul II states, "The 'sovereignty' of the family is essential for the good of society. A truly sovereign and spiritually vigorous nation is always made up of strong families who are aware of their vocation and mission in history.... To relegate [the family] to a subordinate or secondary role, excluding it from its rightful position in society, would be to inflict grave harm on the authentic growth of society as a whole."[2] To weaken the family is to weaken the nation.

The principle of subsidiarity describes the cooperation between families and government. First, the family should do what it can do. Second, what the family cannot do, the township or city government should do. Third, what that level of government cannot do, the state should do. And finally, what the state cannot do, the national government should do. For example, the Hahn family can build a driveway but not a road; the state can have a militia but not an army. Every entity has a role, provided this principle of subsidiarity is honored.

Pope Benedict XVI concurs: "We do not need a State which regulates and controls everything, but a State which, in accordance with the principle of subsidiarity, generously acknowledges and supports initiatives arising from the different social forces and combines spontaneity with closeness to those in need."[3] In other words, legislators should welcome initiatives that strengthen families, because strong families make a strong culture.

FAMILIES RENEW SOCIETY

Prayer and fasting. Blessed Pope John Paul II wrote, "Families are meant to contribute to the transformation of the earth and the renewal of the world, of creation and of all humanity."[4] Part of that renewal is through prayer; part of that renewal is through action.

We pray that our leaders be people of integrity and govern with wisdom and justice. We pray that God will call godly men and women to political leadership in our society and perhaps we even listen for that call ourselves. We pray for greater understanding so that we can contribute to our society. We pray for the preservation of the sanctity of marriage and the protection of human life from conception to natural death.

Where our country has strayed from God's standard of righteousness, we pray, with fasting, for forgiveness. "If my people who are called by my name humble themselves and pray and seek my face, and turn from their wicked ways, then I will hear from heaven, and will forgive their sin and heal their land" (2 Chronicles 7:14).

Raise a godly family. In 2004 several articles accused "conservative, religiously minded Americans" of "putting far more of their genes into the future than their liberal, secular counterparts."[5] In other words, we are having babies and raising them to be pro-life!

Many Christians—some call them "natalists"—"are more spiritually, emotionally and physically invested in their homes than in any other sphere of life, having concluded that parenthood is the most enriching and elevating thing they can do."[6] This is primarily a spiritual rather than a political movement, though it will have political consequences. I want a bumper sticker that reads, "I have six children, and they will vote!"

Opportunities for public service. People of influence need to do the good they can in public life. The husband of the Proverbs 31 woman is honored as a leader of influence. "Her husband is known in the gates, when he sits among the elders of the land" (Proverbs 31:23). We women have opportunities to serve publicly as well as enable our husbands to serve.

We must take a strong stand for community values, opposing the damaging effects of abortion and pornography on marriages and families. Though the Church is not political, she always promotes the dignity of the person and the dignity of marriage in each society in which she has been planted. Pope Benedict XVI says, "The direct duty to work for a just ordering of society…is proper to the lay faithful. As citizens of the State, they are called to take part in public life in a personal capacity."[7]

We should join other like-minded individuals and act in concert as lay faithful. "By fulfilling their civic duties, guided by a Christian conscience, in conformity with its values, the lay faithful exercise their proper task of infusing the temporal order with Christian values,…cooperating with other citizens according to their particular competence and responsibility."[8]

How can we encourage more people to be civic-minded? What leadership and vision can we provide, with minimal time for maximum impact? How can we engage our teens in the process?

In the 2008 presidential election, students attending Catholic high schools in Dayton, Ohio, circulated petitions that stated, "We the undersigned are pro-life. We will be voting in the next presidential election, and we want you to know we are here." They collected thousands of signatures, serving notice to various presidential candidates. What a powerful statement! The next generation will make a difference.

Catholic social teaching provides guidance as to what is just, given the political and economic issues of the day. The Church "cannot and must not replace the State."[9] However, the Church's role is indispensable in helping us understand the principles that guide us.

Do you vote? If you do not vote because you do not know the candidates, get to know them, and get to know the issues. Your county board of elections will give you a sample ballot (available online). Examine candidates' voting records and endorsements. In our American society it is a privilege and a responsibility to be involved in the election process.

Some people claim that voting pro-life is single-issue voting. I think being pro-life is a qualification to run for office. Abortion is *not* an issue, and it certainly is *not* health care!

Can you imagine a politician being taken seriously should he represent all of the people in his district *except* Hispanics? Or people over the age of sixty-five? Or people with handicaps? Politicians cannot choose which segments of the populace they will represent. Let's have all pro-life candidates, and *then* we will discuss issues.

When Pope Paul VI addressed the United Nations, he said, "Respect for life, even with regard to the great problem of birth, should find here in Your Assembly its highest affirmation and its most reasoned defense. You must strive to multiply bread so that it suffices for the tables of mankind, and not favor an artificial control of birth, which would be irrational, in order to diminish the number of guests at the banquet of life."[10] What a bold proclamation!

We witness about the civilization of love and life to our culture through our families. "However, the family remains *vulnerable* and can easily fall prey to dangers which weaken it or actually destroy its unity and stability. As a result of these dangers families cease to be witnesses of the civilization of love and can even become a negation of it, a kind of *countersign*."[11] More desperately than we know, our culture and future generations need us to be faithful.

We must speak for those who cannot, and we call on our leaders to do the same. The queen mother of King Lemuel, tells her son, "Open your mouth for the mute, for the rights of all who are left desolate. Open your mouth, judge righteously, maintain the rights of the poor and needy" (Proverbs 31:8–9).

We do not substitute prayer for action. We pray, and then we act. The prophet Micah says, "He has showed you, O man, what is good; and what does the LORD require of you but to do justice, and to love kindness, and to walk humbly with your God" (Micah 6:8). We must remain vigilant. "Give justice to the weak and the fatherless; maintain the right of the afflicted and the destitute. Rescue the weak and the needy; deliver them from the hand of the wicked" (Psalm 82:3–4).

During the time of Israel's dispersion in Persia, the king of Persia selected Esther to be his queen. Unbeknownst to him, Esther was a Jew. When the king signed a decree allowing Persians to kill the Jews, Queen Esther was asked to risk her life to reveal that plot to the king. "Who knows whether you have come to the kingdom for such a time as this?" (Esther 4:14). Esther took the risk and saved her people.

This is *our* time in history. This is when God asks us to stand for truth and righteousness and justice. Will we combine prayer with action and bring truth to bear in our culture?

PERIPHERY #4—HAVING CHRIST'S HEART FOR THE WORLD

The Great Commission. Just before his ascension Jesus commissioned his disciples: "All authority in heaven and on earth has been given to me. Go therefore and make disciples of all nations, baptizing them in the name of the Father and of the Son and of the Holy Spirit, teaching them to observe all that I have commanded you; and behold, I am with you always, to the close of the age" (Matthew 28:18–20).

There are three points for us to consider:

First, Jesus is the one with the authority to send us forth as his ambassadors. We cannot make people Christians, but we can share the faith and allow the Spirit to work through his Word in bringing people to faith.

Blessed Pope John Paul II addressed the mistaken notion that taking the gospel to the world was only for clergy. "In the Exhortation *Christifideles Laici,* I spoke explicitly of the Church's 'permanent mission of bringing the Gospel to the multitudes—the millions and millions of men and women—who as yet do not know Christ the Redeemer of humanity,' and of the responsibility of the lay faithful in this regard. The mission *ad gentes* [to the peoples] is incumbent upon the entire People of God."[12]

Second, we must catechize people once they are baptized. We are to teach them the fullness of the faith. This means we are committed to lifelong catechesis.

Third, Jesus has promised us his presence and his power. He is looking for someone, like Mary, who humbly says, "I'm available." Jesus will lead us all, and he will call some to leave their homeland to take the gospel into the world.

I was struggling with leaving my family for two days to speak in St. Louis. I told my son Gabriel, then eight, who was in the front yard playing with a magnifying glass, "I really don't want to leave the family, but I said I would go."

"You have to," he stated matter-of-factly.

That caught me off guard. "I do?"

"Mom, you have to be like a magnifying glass and set people's hearts on fire for Jesus!"

"Thanks, Gabriel!"

What stops us from sharing about Christ? First, we do not share or do not share well because of a lack of love. On the one hand, some people have the Little Bo Peep Syndrome toward those who have been exposed to the faith: Leave them alone, and they will come home. We do not want to make anyone uncomfortable. Do we care that some people have never heard about Jesus? Or that others have drifted from the faith of their childhood and may become so lost that they do not know the way back?

On the other hand, we can become theological pit bulls, ready to take on all comers. That is not the point either. We want to share the truth, but we are not out to destroy.

Second, we do not share out of fear. We fear failure, but we are not required to be successful. In Blessed Mother Teresa's words, "God has not called me to be successful; He has called me to be faithful."[13] We also fear the unknown: How will people react? What will they think of me?

Third, we have excuses: I am too old to learn how to share, or I am too young to evangelize, or I am not well enough to witness. But I have to share who Jesus is and what he has done. Jesus saved *us*, and we were not any more savable than anyone else. We might assume that someone will never become a Christian. That, however, is not for us to decide.

Sometimes people claim that they have a wordless witness, but that is not good enough because our lives are not good enough. Do people at work know that you are a Christian? Are you a person of character and integrity? And at the appropriate time, without misusing time for work, do you share your faith with coworkers? Remember, we were thirsty people who have found Jesus, the living water. We want to point others to the fountain of life.

Jesus said, "You are the salt of the earth" (Matthew 5:13a). Salt adds flavor and preserves food, but it also makes you thirsty for something more. You may go to a film and only want to buy popcorn. But halfway through the movie, you buy a soda because you are thirsty. Pray about being salt, and ask God to make you like movie popcorn salt, so that others will become thirsty to know Christ.

Jesus also said, "You are the light of the world.... Let your light so shine before men, that they may see your good works and give glory to your Father who is in heaven" (Matthew 5:14a, 16). Shine—not shout—so that others may come out of darkness. Is hell real? Care enough to share with others so that that will not be their destination. Is heaven real? Love others enough to want to share eternity with them in heaven.

SUPPORT THE WORK OF MISSIONS

Pray. For more than twenty years we have prayed with our children for the countries of the world when we gather for family devotions each morning. We began about four months before the Iron Curtain fell. As countries shattered the shackles of communism, I was stunned. Day after day we would hear more exciting news, and I would exclaim, "Michael and Gabriel, this is phenomenal!" They did not know how to respond.

One day I noticed that Michael's face looked rather blasé. I asked, "Do you know what this means?"

"I think so."

"Michael, this is the culmination of seventy years of entrenched atheism we thought might never end. Aren't you amazed?"

His answer was simple. "Well, we prayed."

His child's heart thought, "I prayed, and God answered my prayer." He was right, though his prayers echoed decades of prayers throughout the world for liberation that had finally come.

We have prayed "to foster the birth and growth of *vocation*, both priestly and religious as well as in the lay state, *specifically directed to the missions.*"[14] We have learned about saints who were missionaries and been enthralled with their adventures as they took the gospel throughout the world—like St. Ignatius of Loyola, who went to Japan; St. Patrick, who went to Ireland; the North American Martyrs, who witnessed to the Iroquois Indians; and Venerable John, who went to China, just to mention a few. What motivated them? How did they find others who shared that passion?

St. Thérèse of Lisieux is the patron saint of missions, though ironically, she was a young cloistered nun. What she could do was pray for hours, and through her prayers God released power for missionaries.

Meet missionaries. Get to know missionaries, and offer them hospitality when they come to town. Ask for their specific prayer concerns, and stay in touch. Send books or supplies to foreign seminaries, or meet some other specific need. Dollars might stretch farther if missionaries purchase goods where they serve. A thousand dollars paid for an entire year of medical school for a Sudanese man who wanted to do medical missions in his homeland.

Go on a short-term mission. You might consider chaperoning a youth mission trip. Or you could participate in a medical mission if you have training in medicine or dentistry. Every spring break hundreds of Franciscan University students do beach ministry, short-term missions, or a mission in downtown Steubenville.

Family Missions Company (FMC) was founded by Frank and Genie Summers as a Catholic apostolate. For decades the Summerses traveled abroad doing missions with their growing family. In 2000 they established Big Woods Mission in Abbeville, Louisiana, as a place for training missionaries in preparation for foreign missionary work. Following this formation, FMC sends single people and families on short- and long-term missions all over the world.[15]

PILGRIMAGE TO THE NEW JERUSALEM

Heaven is our home. We are sojourners; this is not our home. As my husband frequently says, "We're really here to get out of here. This world is a saint-making machine." Since this life is brief, are we living each day in light of eternity?

We have been baptized into the threefold mission of Christ: We share Christ's *priesthood* as we offer our lives in union with his self-offering in the Mass, consecrating the world to the Father. We continue Christ's *prophetic* witness by responding to the gospel with faith in ongoing conversion and by proclaiming the gospel through our words and actions. And we extend Christ's *kingship* through our acts of charity and pursuit of justice. In this we sanctify the temporal order; we are in the world but not of it.

Harness the hosts of heaven. We are not alone. Not only do we have Christ's promised presence until the close of the age, but he has made possible the communion of saints. "Therefore, since we are surrounded by so great a crowd of witnesses, let us also lay aside every weight, and sin which clings so closely, and let us run with perseverance the race that is set before us, looking to Jesus, the pioneer and perfecter of our faith" (Hebrews 12:1–2).

Notice the present perfect tense: We "are surrounded." That means the saints are with us and will continue to be with us. The setting is like an Olympic stadium in which the people in the stands have all medaled in the race in which we are competing.

What are the witnesses doing? They are not looking at us with disdain, standing in judgment of our poor performance. They know what it takes to run with perseverance. They are with us, praying for us, cheering us on. These older brothers and sisters in Christ are our prayer warriors.

We are in the midst of spiritual warfare. Through prayer we marshal heavenly forces to help us do battle as the Church militant on earth. The St. Michael prayer is powerful, acknowledging his role in leading the armies of angels to assist us. The guardian angel prayer petitions our specific angel. The rosary unites us to the heart of Mary while we reflect on the mysteries of God's work in and through her and her son.

By the grace of God and the power of the Spirit, we can fulfill the Great Commission Jesus gave his disciples. We are to go throughout the world and proclaim the gospel, baptizing and catechizing people in every nation. Whether we witness in our extended family, neighborhood, parish, country, or world, we have a mission to live and to proclaim.

CHAPTER FIFTEEN

In Praise of Humility

The Proverbs 31 woman is a woman who fears the Lord. "Charm is deceitful and beauty is vain, but a woman who fears the LORD is to be praised. Give her of the fruit of her hands, and let her works praise her in the gates" (Proverbs 31:30–31).

Only a few women are flawless beauties, but all women can have the inner beauty of godliness. Sickness, accidents, and old age might mar good looks, but these challenges can even increase the loveliness of a soul. Charm and beauty are fading qualities, but a humble fear of the Lord lasts forever.

Humility is the crown of a godly woman's character. "The fear of the LORD is instruction in wisdom, and humility goes before honor" (Proverbs 15:33; see 18:12; 22:4). Humility comes first; praise follows. "Clothe yourselves, all of you, with humility toward one another, for 'God opposes the proud, but gives grace to the humble.' Humble yourselves therefore under the mighty hand of God, that in due time he may exalt you" (1 Peter 5:5–6; see James 4:10).

"Let another praise you and not your own mouth" (Proverbs 27:2). The Proverbs 31 woman is not the one trumpeting how well she has done. Her husband, who knows her best, and her children honor her publicly. False humility dishonors God, who gives the gifts, talents, and abilities. True humility accepts others' praise graciously, acknowledging God as the source of all that is good.

Jesus exemplified humility and called his disciples to imitate his example: "He who is greatest among you shall be your servant; whoever exalts himself will be humbled, and whoever humbles himself will be exalted" (Matthew 23:11–12).

Blessed Mother Teresa of Calcutta was scheduled to speak at a conference that my father organized in Washington, D.C. When she had to cancel, due to health reasons, my father asked her, "Mother, how can we pray for you?"

She did not ask for prayers for her order or her health. She simply asked, "Pray that I not spoil God's work." What a humble response!

Blessed Pope John Paul II went from being a robust athlete to being a man who could not stand upright and had to wipe drool from his mouth. He could have withdrawn into his private quarters but instead chose to show us how to age and how to die. He embraced the humiliation of being ill and dying in front of the world. His humility drew our hearts closer to the Lord.

CATCH THE VISION FOR YOUR VOCATION

Jesus wants you to have the hope that grace is at work in ways you do not see. He wants you to look beyond the visible to the greater invisible reality of what he is doing in and through your marriage and family. This spiritual dimension is every bit as real as your daily experiences.

If we, like St. Peter walking on water, take our eyes off Jesus, we begin to sink under the weight of our flaws, failures, and lack of faith (see Matthew 14:22–33). Blessed Pope John Paul II exhorts us:

Do not be afraid of the risks! God's strength is always far more powerful than your difficulties! Immeasurably greater than the evil at work in the world is the power of the Sacrament of Reconciliation, which the Fathers of the Church rightly called a "second Baptism." Much more influential than the corruption present in the world is the divine power of the Sacrament of Confirmation, which brings Baptism to its maturity. And incomparably greater than all is the power of the Eucharist.[1]

Through the sacraments our faith is strengthened, and our vision for God's plan for our lives is renewed.

The disparity between the ideal we envision for our marriage and family life and the reality of our experience can be overwhelming. This is especially true when we fall into the trap of comparing our family to other families. You and I need to remember that our Lord says to us what we would say to our toddler who stumbles: "My precious daughter, I love you! Just take another step." Each day can be a new beginning, a fresh start.

When we feel weak, we recall Jesus' words, "My grace is sufficient for you, for my power is made perfect in weakness" (2 Corinthians 12:9). When we feel inadequate, we remember Mary's humble response, "Behold, I am the handmaid of the Lord; let it be to me according to your word" (Luke 1:38). When we feel anxious, we bring our concerns to the one who has called us into this marvelous vocation; he will give us his peace (see Philippians 4:6–7).

If we yield our hearts and our homes to the Lord, he will show us the path of holiness that runs through our vocation. He will lead us to himself and show us how we can lead our family to him. The Lord will reveal to the world his relationship to the Church through our earthly marriage.

The Proverbs 31 woman helps us experience the fruit of life-nurturing love. This love produces holiness for our souls, well-being for our spouse and children, justice and peace for our country, and salvation for the world. Let's pray for each other, that God's grace may produce this fruit in each of our lives.

Appendix A—Video Outlines

Session One: "She Opens Her Hand to the Poor" (Proverbs 31:20)

I. Introduction (Proverbs 31:10–12)

II. Diligence in charity

    A. Personal involvement (Proverbs 31:20)

        1. Timely hands-on care

        2. Timeless perspective (Matthew 6:19–21)

        3. Goal of earning includes being generous (Ephesians 4:28; Proverbs 3:9–10)

    B. Called to give

        1. Act of faith (Proverbs 3:9–10)

        2. Act of worship (1 Corinthians 16:2)

        3. Expression of gratitude (Proverbs 22:9)

        4. Matter of obedience (see Matthew 6:2–4; Luke 6:38; Proverbs 11:24–25, 28; Ezekiel 16:49)

    C. Acts of charity

        1. Empower our prayers (Isaiah 58:6–9)

        2. Weaken the power of money over us (see 1 Timothy 6:6–10)

        3. Even punish our enemies (Proverbs 25:21–22)

III. Awareness of the needs around us

    A. Open our eyes to the needs of the poor (Proverbs 28:27; 19:17)

    B. Open our ears to the cries of the poor (Proverbs 21:13)

    C. Open our hearts to the poor with compassion

        1. First priority: your household (1 Timothy 5:4, 8)

        2. Second priority: the household of faith (Galatians 6:10; James 2:15–17)

        3. Third priority: sojourner, fatherless, widow (see Deuteronomy 24:19–22; James 1:27)

        4. Fourth priority: others in need around us

IV. How should we give? (2 Corinthians 9:6–15)

    A. Generously (Luke 9:12–17; 21:1–4; 2 Corinthians 8:2–5)

    B. Freely

    C. Cheerfully (Psalm 37:25–26)

    D. Respectfully (Proverbs 14:31)

V. Works of mercy (Matthew 25:34–36, 40

    A. Feed the hungry

        1. Hospitality in your home

         a) Not the same as entertaining (Romans 12:13)

         b) Invitations to whom? (Luke 14:13–14; Hebrews 13:2)

         c) Gather at table (Sirach 9:15–16; 1 Peter 4:9)

        2. Feed those outside your home

    B. Give a drink to the thirsty

    C. Clothe the naked

    D. Shelter the homeless

        1. Foster care or adoption

        2. Shelter sojourners

        3. Multigenerational living

        4. Radical hospitality (Sirach 11:29)

        5. Work on a home-build (Sirach 29:21–22)

    E. Visit the sick and imprisoned

    F. Ransom the captive

    G. Bury the dead

VI. Desire to be rich in mercy

    A. Jesus' example (2 Corinthians 8:9)

    B. A word to the poor: receive graciously

    C. A word to the rich: give generously (1 Timothy 6:17–19)

SESSION TWO: THE PARENTING ADVENTURE: TEENS
(PROVERBS 31:27)

I. Our attitude toward our teens

   A. Each child is a gift from God

   B. Anticipate delight or disaster?

   C. Similarities between teens and twos

   D. All grown up…almost

   E. Celebrate the milestones

II. Nurture the soul of your teen

   A. Challenge him to choose Christ daily (John 15:13–14)

   B. Share the sacraments

   C. Study the Word (Psalm 119:105)

   D. Do apologetics (see Romans 1:18–20; 1 Peter 3:15; Ephesians 4:14)

   E. Develop habits of holiness

   F. Nurture a sense of vocation (Proverbs 18:22; 1 Corinthians 7:32b–34a)

   G. Trust God; he has a plan!

III. Relationships with siblings

   A. Preparation for marriage

   B. Deep attachments of the heart (Proverbs 3:27)

     1. Words of affirmation

     2. Quality time together

     3. Acts of service

     4. Gift giving

     5. Physical touch and closeness

   C. Conflict resolution (1 Corinthians 13:4–7)

     1. Teens: Watch your words (Proverbs 11:13; Proverbs 10:19; see 6:16–19)

     2. Teens: Watch your anger (Proverbs 16:32)

        3. Parents: Know when to intervene (Proverbs 18:19)

    D. Develop a strong family culture (Romans 12:9–10)

IV. Nurture teen toward overall maturity (Proverbs 24:13–14)

    A. Personal skills (Proverbs 5:23)

    B. Intellectual skills

    C. Life skills through health education at home

    D. Financial skills

    E. Social skills

V. Beginning the journey into adulthood

    A. Recognize growing independence (Matthew 25:21)

    B. God's example—discipline demonstrates love (Proverbs 3:11, 12; see Hebrews 12:3–11; Sirach 26:10)

    C. Be diligent (Proverbs 29:17; Sirach 7:23–24; Proverbs 28:13)

    D. Apply moral standard to all

    E. Appeal process

    F. Day of Jubilee

    G. Keep parenting! (see Luke 2:50–52)

    H. Honor is key (Ephesians 6:2; see Exodus 20:12)

    I. Works of mercy applied to teens—see chapter four

VI. Setting CLEAR boundaries for teens

    A. CLEAR boundaries

        1. Consistent

        2. Limits that are reasonable

        3. Enforceable consequences

        4. Adjusted as needed

        5. Responsibilities linked to privileges

    B. Bedtimes and curfews

    C. Family policies on media (see 1 Peter 5:7–8)—see chapter four

VII. Rebellion

    A. Teens rebel against relationships (Ezzos) (Proverbs 19:18; 29:17)

    B. Broken relationships are painful (Psalm 4:4)

    C. Mary, Undoer of Knots

    D. Choice: Will I dig a pit or a well? (see Proverbs 26:27)

    E. Prepare to welcome back with forgiveness (see Luke 15:11–32)

    F. Great is God's faithfulness (Lamentations 3:22–23)

Session Three: The Virtue of Friendship (Proverbs 31:27b)

I. Qualities of true friends (*CCC,* 2347; Proverbs 13:20)

    A. Choose friends wisely (Proverbs 13:20; see Proverbs 22:24–25; 1 Corinthians 5:9–11)

    B. Is consistent (Proverbs 17:17)

    C. Is trustworthy (Proverbs 18:24)

    D. Forgives (Proverbs 17:9; Luke 17:3–4)

    E. Tells the truth (Proverbs 27:6; Ephesians 4:29)

    F. Is empathetic (Romans 12:15)

    G. Challenges us (Proverbs 27:17)

    H. Is a gift from God (Sirach 6:14–16)

    I. Saints have saints for companions

II. The virtue of chastity

    A. What is chastity? (*CCC,* 2345)

    B. Flee fornication (1 Corinthians 6:18)

    C. Exercise self-control (Song of Solomon 2:7; 3:5)

    D. Worth the wait (1 Thessalonians 4:3–5)

    E. Honor future spouse (Proverbs 31:12)

    F. Purity

        1. Of heart (2 Timothy 2:22; see *CCC,* 2521)

      2. In mind (Psalm 119:9, 11; see Matthew 5:27–28; 2 Corinthians 10:5; Philippians 4:8)

      3. Of intention—self-mastery (Proverbs 11:22; 1 Timothy 4:12)

      4. Of affection (Ecclesiastes 3:1, 5a)

      5. Of dress

      6. Power of purity

      7. Accountability

III. Life-changing choices (*CCC,* 1632)

IV. Typical American dating for teens

    A. Dating is just for fun

    B. Age doesn't matter (but maturity does)

    C. Dating helps you figure out what you want and don't want

    D. Dating involves many relationships

    E. Dating focuses on externals: looks, clothes, popularity

    F. Romance often precedes friendship

    G. Feelings get ahead of clear thinking

    H. Dating can be isolating

    I. Dating occurs with limited parental input

V. An alternative: honorable courtship

    A. Word picture: a castle

    B. Rebuild where necessary (Proverbs 24:30–34)

    C. Preparation: no passive parenting

    D. What is courtship?

    E. What if courtship doesn't work?

VI. Building solid friendships (same sex; opposite sex)

    A. How teens develop friendships

      1. Serve together

      2. Work together

      3. Play together

4. Pray together

5. Serve one another (see Galatians 5:13)

6. Enjoy each other

7. Love each other (Romans 12:9)

8. Reach out to include others

B. Parents' role in their teen's friendships (Proverbs 22:11)

   1. Explain family rules so teen knows parents' expectations

   2. Create environment and opportunities for wholesome friendships

   3. Continue to parent while developing friendship with your teen

   4. Pray through the process

SESSION FOUR: PARENTING ADULT CHILDREN (PROVERBS 31:28A)

I. They call her blessed

A. For raising godly children in an ungodly culture (Genesis 6:5; Hebrews 11:7)

B. For their good name (Proverbs 10:7; 22:1)

C. For blessing they receive through their parents' obedience (Exodus 20:5–6; 1 Peter 3:7)

D. For her prayers (Hebrews 7:25)

   1. Specific concerns (see Hebrews 7:25)

   2. Safety from physical or spiritual harm (see Job 1:5, 10)

   3. Godly spouse for a child (see Sirach 7:25; 2 Corinthians 6:14–15)

   4. Preparations for a child's life's work (Proverbs 24:27)

II. Adult-to-adult communication

A. Communicating love and respect

B. Having courage to let control of the relationship shift

C. Loving from a distance

D. Moving back home—see chapter seven

E. Young adults must honor their parents (*CCC*, 2217–2218; Proverbs 23:22; see Sirach 7:27–28)

III. Advice to a young adult: Live your singleness richly

A. Be patient

B. Pray for your future spouse

C. Thank God always (Nehemiah 8:10; 1 Thessalonians 5:16–18)

D. Marriage: a particular call

E. Questions to ask before you court—see chapter eight

IV. Honorable courtship

A. Is courtship possible?

B. Ask her father

C. How do you court?

D. Accountability (Proverbs 11:14; Psalm 37:4–5)

E. Questions to ask before engagement—see chapter eight

V. Engagement

A. A time of transition

B. A time of peace

C. A time of celebration

D. A time of preparation (*CCC*, 1632)

   1. Prepare to leave (Genesis 2:24)

   2. Prepare to cleave

   3. Prepare to become one flesh

E. No cohabitation

   1. Freedom without responsibility

   2. Can't "practice" a sacrament

   3. Avoid appearance of evil (1 Thessalonians 5:22)

   4. Tough love

VI. A time to gather and a time to scatter

    A. A sense of loss as well as gain (Psalm 30:11–12)

    B. Spiritual warfare (John 16:33)

    C. Art of interpretation

VII. One amazing day

    A. But only one day

    B. Honor all involved

    C. Avoid debt

    D. Be inclusive

    E. Everyone is ready (2 Corinthians 10:3)

VIII. Wedding Day

    A. The power of the sacrament

    B. Mass—a fitting context (*CCC*, 1621)

    C. Reception—a couple's first act of hospitality

    D. Honeymoon—rest and relax

SESSION FIVE: CONSOLIDATING OUR GAINS AS A GROWING FAMILY (PROVERBS 31:28B)

I. New role: mother-in-law

    A. Mary as our mother-in-law

    B. What's in a name?—see chapter ten

    C. Clash of the Titans or merging of the meek?

    D. Patron saints for in-laws

II. The dance of an "altared" relationship

    A. A new relationship

    B. We don't have a past yet

    C. Live love deeply (1 John 3:18)

    D. Include each in-law fully

    E. Homecoming—see chapter ten

    F. Visit them in their home

III. New roles for siblings
    A. Honor and respect
        1. For siblings left behind
        2. For the sibling who wed
    B. Keep siblings' hearts open to each other
    C. Plan family times that include the new couple

IV. Encourage newlyweds as they forge a new family
    A. Where to live?
    B. Which traditions?
    C. The priority of each other's families

V. Risk love (1 Corinthians 13:7)
    A. Love bears all things
    B. Love believes all things
    C. Love hopes all things
    D. Love endures all things (Romans 8:26)
    E. Way of the Cross for mothers and mothers-in-law
    F. Build up instead of tear down (Romans 8:28)
    G. Fruit of humility: Naomi and Ruth (see Ruth 4:15);
       Jethro and Moses (Exodus 18:1–24)

VI. Undergird each married couple
    A. Mentoring (Titus 2:4–5)
        1. Mothering the mothers (see Isaiah 40:11)
        2. Mothering the fathers
        3. Expressing gratitude for them
    B. Money (*CCC,* 2230)

VII. Generation to generation
    A. God is faithful (Psalm 100:5; Isaiah 59: 21)
    B. Proclaim his faithfulness to the next generation (Psalm 78:4–8; see Psalm 71:5, 18; 89:1)
    C. Respond with faithfulness (Psalm 103:17–18)
    D. The power of a praying grandparent (2 Timothy 1:5)

VIII. Grandparenting, a new experience of grace (Proverbs 17:6)

    A. Welcome new grandmothers

    B. Pray to be unselfish

    C. Embrace the task God is giving you

    D. The influence of grandparents

    E. Our goals as grandparents

        1. Share our wisdom (Proverbs 4:3–6)

        2. Share our wealth (Proverbs 13:22; 2 Corinthians 12:14)

        3. Share our wonder at God's goodness

Session Six: Witness to the World
(Proverbs 31:29–31)

I.   Priorities (Proverbs 31:29)

    A. The core: world within, world without

    B. The periphery: world within, world without (Romans 13:8)

    C. Balancing priorities

    D. Jesus' call to witness to the world (Acts 1:8)

II.   Jerusalem: parish (Psalm 40:10; Acts 2:42)

    A. Adult faith formation—www.salvationhistory.com

    B. Fellowship

        1. Share your time

        2. Share your treasure

        3. Share your talents (see 1 Corinthians 12:4–11; Romans 12:4–8)

    C. Breaking bread: the Eucharist

    D. Prayer (see Matthew 14:23; Luke 4:40-44)

    E. Care for priests, religious, missionaries

    F. Godchildren

    G. What's a contemplative to do?

III. Judea: neighbors
    A. Our extended family
    B. The people we live near
        1. Bring Jesus to our neighbors
        2. Notice our neighbors' needs (Proverbs 27:10–11)
        3. Befriend our neighbors (see Sirach 9:14; 31:15; Proverbs 11:12–13; 25:17; Ephesians 5:25)
    C. Those in need
IV. Samaria: our society
    A. Share God's Word (Romans 13:1; James 3:17–18)
    B. Express the genius of woman in society
    C. Civic-mindedness
    D. Families as "sovereign" societies
        1. Principle of subsidiarity (2 Chronicles 7:14)
        2. Families' rights and individuals' rights
        3. Families' influence in public affairs (Proverbs 31:23; see Esther 4:14)
        4. Justice for the poor (Proverbs 31:8, 9; see 29:7; Psalm 82:3–4)
        5. Natalism
V. Ends of the earth: the world
    A. The Great Commission (Matthew 28:18–20)
    B. What stops us from sharing about Christ?
    C. Support for missions
        1. Prayer
        2. Get to know saints who were missionaries
        3. Get to know current missionaries
        4. Consider a short-term mission trip
VI. The New Jerusalem
    A. Heaven is our home
    B. Harness the host of heaven (Hebrews 12:1–2)

VII. Humility (Proverbs 31:30–31)

    A. Fear of the Lord (Proverbs 15:33)

    B. "Humility is the foundation of prayer." (*CCC*, 2559)

    C. With humility she accepts praise (Proverbs 27:2)

    D. Humility has its rewards (James 4:10; Proverbs 22:4)

    E. Humility of her service imitates Jesus (Matthew 23:11–12)

VIII. Catch the vision

Appendix B

Questions for an Intergenerational Women's Study

When you break into small groups, you can begin with either, "Was there anything particularly new to you?" or, "Look over the questions, and select what you would like to talk about."

The first group of questions is recommended for group discussion. The second group is more suitable for personal reflection and possibly journaling.

Questions can apply in different ways, depending on each woman's stage in life. For example, a woman might respond based on her relationship with her parents-in-law rather than as a mother-in-law, if she is not at that stage yet. She might talk about her own grandparents rather than about being a grandparent.

Session One: She Opens Her Hand to the Poor

1. What are some ways you balance your priorities?
2. What are some things you do to keep from feeling overwhelmed?
3. What are some ways you can be more personally involved in your giving?
4. Is it OK to make a gift anonymously? Is it advisable?
5. How do acts of charity lessen the power of money in our lives?
6. Is it sinful to be rich? To want to be rich?
7. How can we help each other become more sensitive to others' needs?
8. Is there a different obligation to our brothers and sisters in Christ, before the needs of the rest of the world?
9. Do we see our possessions as belonging to God, on loan to us? How does that alter our perspective and how we act?
10. How are you performing works of mercy as a family?
***

1. What are the differences between the communal living of Jerusalem and communism?
2. What can I do this week to show personal compassion to the poor in my area?
3. What does my husband think we could do?
4. Can I involve my children more directly in caring for the poor?

SESSION 2: The Parenting Adventure: Teens

1. What is your attitude toward the teen years? Does that reflect how you experienced the teen years?
2. What is the difference between being your teen's parent and being your teen's friend?
3. What are ways a strong family identity can help your kids navigate the teen years?
4. How can you help your teens build stronger relationships with siblings?
5. How can you parent teens in the strength of the Lord instead of on your own?

***

1. Have you heard about the appeal process? Would that work in your family to diminish conflict?
2. How do you serve your teens?
3. Is there pain right now in a relationship with a teenaged child that you need to bring under the shadow of the cross?
4. What boundaries have you set for your teens concerning media? Have you and your husband set a policy together?

SESSION 3: The Virtue of Friendship

1. How important are friendships for your teens? How can they be positive influences on your children's lives?
2. How can you help your teens work harder on friendships with immediate and extended family?
3. Have you discussed qualities of a good friend with your teen?

4. What is the difference between friendliness (something we show to all people) and developing a friendship (intimacy with a few like-minded and like-hearted people)?

5. What do Jesus' words from the Our Father mean: "Lead us not into temptation but deliver us from evil"? How does this relate to avoiding the near occasion of sin?

6. Why do older people often say to mothers of younger children, "Little people equal little problems; big people equal big problems"?

7. Have you discussed with your teen the difference between typical dating and developing deeper friendships during the high school years?

8. How can you encourage your teen to develop a relationship with the Church?

***

1. The virtues that assist our children to resist negative peer pressure include fear of God, respect for parents and others in authority, a healthy relationship with their parents, an internalized faith with an understanding of right and wrong, wisdom, independent thinking, self-control, and a sense of personal accomplishment in at least one area of talent or skill. Select one of these areas for each of your teens for prayers and then guidance.

2. Talk with your teens about the influence of friends. What would they do if they were tempted? As in sports, the best defense is a good offense!

3. Bring a teen to the standard: God's Word.
   a. Drinking (Galatians 5:19, 21)
   b. Foul talk (Ephesians 4:29; 2 Timothy 2:16; James 5:10)
   c. Pressure to follow the crowd (Exodus 23:2)
   d. Premarital sex (1 Thessalonians 4:3–6)

4. Look up passages that apply to parents and teens. It might be interesting to look at them with your teen and ask him or her how the passages apply to both of you:
   a. Romans 13:8; 14:13;15:7, 14

b. Hebrews 3:13; 10:24
c. Ephesians 4:2, 32
d. Colossians 3:16
e. 1 Peter 1:22
f. 1 John 3:11; 4:7, 11

SESSION 4: Parenting Adult Children
1. Why is having a good name important?
2. How can you pray for your children's future spouses and their families?
3. How have your communications with your adult children matured?
4. How does your marriage strengthen your adult children?
5. How can young adults live their singleness in a way that is joyful and beautiful? How can we guide them?
6. Why is cohabitation wrong?
7. How has engagement been an adjustment for your family?
8. How can you help your young adults prepare more for their marriage than for their wedding day?

***

1. How can you undergird young adults without crowding them? How have your parents or in-laws done this?
2. Do you have any new insights from Noah and his family?
3. What do young adults continue to owe their parents?
4. Why is spiritual warfare an element of a couple's preparing for a godly marriage?
5. Wedding costs—are they worth going into debt?

SESSION 5: Consolidating Our Gains as a Growing Family
1. How can you demonstrate respect for the couple as their own new family?
2. How can you strengthen siblings' relationships in the family after the wedding?
3. What is involved in loving an in-law?

4. What are the differences between having your adult children visit in your home and your visiting them in theirs?

5. How would you describe your grandparents or even your great-grandparents if you knew them?

   a. What impressions did they make?

   b. What do you hope to imitate with your grandchildren?

   c. What do you wish your grandparents had done that you plan to do with your grandchildren?

SESSION 6: Witness to the World

1. What keeps you from witnessing for Christ?

2. How do you balance apostolate through your parish with family commitments?

3. Do you know your neighbors? How have you reached out to them?

4. How do you balance sharing the gospel with providing help for the needy?

5. How do you inspire your children to be mission-minded?

6. Are there particular missions that your family supports?

7. Do politics and your faith mix well?

***

1. Is there an apostolate at your parish in which you would like to serve?

2. Would your spouse be supportive?

3. What could you do to get to know more of your neighbors?

4. How can you help your children be involved in outreach with their friends?

5. How can you share with more women this vision for marriage and family life?

6. How can you strengthen the marriages in your parish?

RADICAL HOSPITALITY: AN INVITATION
TO SHARE LIFE TOGETHER

Extended household is an expression of radical hospitality and sacrificial love. Instead of loving those we feel like loving, we love people with whom we share life.

We all have rough edges that need to be smoothed. In our families we can grow comfortable with our weaknesses, flaws, and failings. In sharing our life with others—eating, talking, working, and praying together—we are on better behavior.

My parents began household living when I, the oldest child, was thirteen. It was an amazing experience to open our home to love and to serve others. The many people who lived with us did not remain the same, nor did we. We were blessed by their gifts of music, laughter, love of sports, and so on. Our family gave them a desire for a godly marriage by showing them how a Christian marriage works. And some grew in a desire to be a pastor like my dad.

Scott and I prayerfully made the decision to welcome students into our family when we moved to Steubenville, Ohio, in 1990. From 1990 through 2010 we have had thirty-five students live with us. We had the space, and the setup gave us more hands to help. It provided additional older brothers and sisters for our children, filled our home with love and laughter, and gave us opportunities to share the joys and challenges of marriage and family life. Through these students the Lord has enriched—and continues to bless—our family.

We have seen extended household as part of our stewardship of the home God has given us: It is his home, to do with as he wills.

MEALS

We shared a dinner hour (6:00–7:00) from Monday through Saturday and lunch on Sunday. Students who had to miss a meal alerted me early enough so I could adjust quantities. Over time we extended invitations to their friends to join us and adjusted for evening classes, date nights, family meals out, and other commitments.

We had an open-fridge, open-pantry policy: People could help themselves, unless it was obvious that food had been set aside for a meal. We provided food from which they could prepare their own breakfasts and lunches. I accommodated preferences but did not prepare separate meals for them or have them cook for themselves. If students brought food into the house—leftovers or groceries—they labeled it for themselves, or it was available to anyone.

RENT

The first few years we asked students for rent. After a while we reduced and then eliminated rent, but we still needed help around the house.

ROOM

We provided a desk, bed, and dresser for each student. We expected the students to keep their rooms neat and clean them once a week with supplies we provided. I took care of cleaning the bathrooms, since all the students did not have the same standard I had.

We also provided soap and toilet paper but not personal items. We provided detergent and dryer sheets for their laundry, as well as the use of an iron and ironing board.

WORK

We enlisted all children old enough and household members for dish duty. The person who cooked was exempt from dish duty that evening.

We also asked each person to contribute five hours of work a week. The tasks varied: painting, wallpapering, carpentry, yard work, building walls, planting a garden or orchard. I set the schedule for work on Sunday evenings for the following week. We adjusted when students had large assignments due or exams.

We asked the students to record their work time and submit their hours monthly. This helped keep them accountable and ensured that we did not take advantage of their generosity. We paid them for any additional work.

VISITING

Our family rule—no friends of the opposite sex in a bedroom—applied to all. Unlike a dorm room, a bedroom is just a bedroom in a home. This rule safeguarded the students and us from inappropriate situations and set a good example for our children. We made space available elsewhere in our home for a couple who wanted to visit.

ALCOHOL

We did not want alcohol kept in students' bedrooms. We limited where alcohol was located, with clear instructions to our children not to imbibe or serve friends.

SUNDAY

Sunday is a day of rest and refreshment. Though we hope our work is enjoyable, we do not work on the Lord's Day. This is a family discipline, and we appreciated the students' support for this.

HOURS

Though students were adults, we requested they be in no later than 2:00 AM, except in unusual circumstances. We asked them to alert us beforehand if they would be out later, so we would not be concerned for their safety. They also needed keys, since doors would be locked.

SHORT ACCOUNTS

We asked the students to let us know—and told them we would let them know—when things were not right between us. For everyone's well-being it was important that we not hold grudges or keep frustrations inside. A simple misunderstanding could become complex unless we talked it through.

This has been an amazing adventure, extending hospitality in a radical way. Once again we have seen that we cannot outgive God as we share our home and resources.

RECOMMENDED RESOURCES

BOOKS

Baker, Robert J., and Benedict J. Groeschel. *When Did We See You, Lord?* Huntington, Ind.: Our Sunday Visitor, 2005.

Benedict XVI. *Deus Caritas Est.* Encyclical Letter on Christian Love. December 25, 2005. www.vatican.va.

Bennett, Art and Laraine. *The Temperament God Gave You: The Classic Key to Knowing Yourself, Getting Along with Others, and Growing Closer to the Lord.* Manchester, N.H.: Sophia, 2005.

Catechism of the Catholic Church, second edition. Vatican City: Libreria Editrice Vaticana, 1997.

Chapman, Annie. *The Mother-in-Law Dance: Can Two Women Love the Same Man and Still Get Along?* Eugene, Oreg.: Harvest, 2004.

Chapman, Gary. *The Five Love Languages: How to Express Heartfelt Commitment to Your Mate.* Chicago: Northfield, 1995.

———. *In-Law Relationships: The Chapman Guide to Becoming Friends with Your In-Laws.* Carol Stream, Ill.: Tyndale, 2008.

Chapman, Gary, and Ross Campbell. *The Five Love Languages of Children.* Chicago: Moody, 1997.

Cloud, Henry, and John Townsend. *Boundaries: When to Say YES, When to Say NO, To Take Control of Your Life.* Grand Rapids: Zondervan, 1992.

Covey, Stephen. *The 7 Habits of Highly Effective Families.* New York: Golden, 1997.

DeMoss, Nancy, and Dannah Gresh. *Lies Young Women Believe and the Truth That Sets Them Free.* Chicago: Moody, 2008.

Elliott, Elisabeth. *The Shaping of a Christian Family: How My Parents Nurtured My Faith.* Grand Rapids: Revell, 1992.

Elwell, Ellen Banks. *The Christian Grandma's Idea Book: Hundreds of Ideas, Tips and Activities to Help You Be a Good Grandma.* Wheaton, Ill.: Crossway, 2008.

Escrivá, Josemaría. *Christ Is Passing By.* Princeton: Scepter, 1973.

Ezzo, Gary and Anne Marie. *Reaching the Heart of Your Teen: Building Relationships That Last a Lifetime.* Chatsworth, Calif.: Growing Families International, 1995.

Fink, John. *Married Saints.* New York: Alba House, 1999.

George, Elizabeth. *God's Wisdom for Little Girls: Virtues and Fun from Proverbs 31.* Eugene, Oreg.: Harvest, 2000.

_____. *God's Wisdom for Little Boys.* Eugene, Oreg.: Harvest, 2002.

Gresh, Dannah. *And the Bride Wore White: Seven Secrets to Sexual Purity.* Chicago: Moody, 2004.

_____. *Secret Keeper: The Delicate Power of Modesty.* Chicago: Moody, 2005.

Hahn, Kimberly. *Beloved and Blessed: Biblical Wisdom for Family Life.* Cincinnati: Servant, 2010.

_____. *Chosen and Cherished: Biblical Wisdom for Your Marriage.* Cincinnati: Servant, 2007.

_____. *Graced and Gifted: Biblical Wisdom for the Homemaker's Heart.* Cincinnati: Servant, 2008.

_____. *Live-Giving Love: Embracing God's Beautiful Design for Marriage.* Cincinnati: Servant, 2001.

Hahn, Kimberly and Scott. *Genesis to Jesus: Studying Scripture from the Heart of the Church.* Cincinnati: Servant, 2010.

Hahn, Kimberly, and Scott Hahn. *Rome Sweet Home: Our Journey to Catholicism.* San Francisco: Ignatius, 1993.

Hahn, Scott. *A Father Who Keeps His Promises.* Cincinnati: Servant, 1998.

_____. *Hope for Hard Times.* Huntington, Ind.: Our Sunday Visitor, 2010.

Harris, Joshua. *Boy Meets Girl.* Sisters, Oreg.: Multnomah, 2000.

_____. *I Kissed Dating Goodbye.* Sisters, Oreg.: Multnomah, 1997.

Hock, Conrad. *The Four Temperaments.* www.angelicum.net.

John Paul II. *Evangelium Vitae.* Encyclical on the Value and Inviolability of Human Life. March 25, 1995. www.vatican.va.

_____. *Gratissimam sane.* Letter to Families. February 2, 1994. www.vatican.va.

Karpen, Cheryl. *Eat Your Peas for My Daughter-in-Law.* Anoka, Minn.: Gently Spoken, 2007.

Leman, Kevin. *The New Birth Order Book: Why You Are the Way You Are.* Grand Rapids: Revell, 1998.

Lewis, C.S. *Mere Christianity.* New York: Macmillan, 1952.

_____. *The Screwtape Letters.* New York: Simon and Schuster, 1996.

Loehr, Gina. *Choosing Beauty: A 30-day Spiritual Makeover for Women.* Cincinnati: Servant, 2009.

_____. *Real Women, Real Saints: Friends for Your Spiritual Journey.* Cincinnati: Servant, 2008.

Martin, Curtis, and Tim Gray. *Boys to Men: The Transforming Power of Virtue.* Steubenville, Ohio: Emmaus Road, 2001.

Martin, Michaelann. *Girls' Night Out: Having Fun with Your Daughter While Raising a Woman of God.* Steubenville, Ohio: Emmaus Road, 2010.

_____. *Woman of Grace: A Bible Study for Married Women.* Steubenville, Ohio: Emmaus Road, 2000.

McCluskey, Christopher and Rachel. *When Two Become One: Achieving Sexual Intimacy in Marriage.* Grand Rapids: Revell, 2004.

Michuta, Gary G. *How to Wolf-Proof Your Kids: A Practical Guide for Keeping Your Kids Catholic.* Wixom, Mich.: Grotto, 2009.

Mitch, Stacy. *Courageous Generosity: A Bible Study for Women on Heroic Sacrifice.* Steubenville, Ohio: Emmaus Road, 2009.

_____. *Courageous Love: A Bible Study on Holiness for Women.* Steubenville, Ohio: Emmaus Road, 1999.

_____. *Courageous Virtue: A Bible Study on Moral Excellence for Women.* Steubenville, Ohio: Emmaus Road, 2000.

_____. *Courageous Women: A Study on the Heroines of Biblical History.* Steubenville, Ohio: Emmaus Road, 2002.

Mugridge, Christine Anne, ed. *God's Call to Women: Twelve Spiritual Memoirs.* Includes chapters by Ronda Chervin, Kimberly Hahn, Chiara Lubich, Susan Muto, Alice von Hildebrand, and others. Cincinnati: Servant, 2003.

Ratzinger, Joseph. "Doctrinal Note on Some Questions Regarding the Participation of Catholics in Political Life." Issued by the Congregation of the Doctrine of the Faith. November 24, 2002.

Scanlan, Michael. *Appointment With God.* Steubenville, Ohio: Franciscan University Press, 1987.

Thigpen, Paul and Leisa. *Building Catholic Family Traditions.* Huntington, Ind.: Our Sunday Visitor, 1999.

Vatican II. *Gaudium et Spes* [Joy and Hope]. December 7, 1965. www.vatican.va.

Von Hildebrand, Alice. *By Love Refined: Letters to a Young Bride.* Manchester, N.H.: Sophia, 1989.

Wilson, Douglas. *Her Hand in Marriage: Biblical Courtship in the Modern World.* Moscow, Idaho: Canon, 1997.

Wood, Stephen. *The ABCs of Choosing a Good Husband: How to Find and Marry a Great Guy.* Port Charlotte, Fla.: Family Life, 2001.

_____. *The ABCs of Choosing a Good Wife: How to Find and Marry a Great Girl.* Port Charlotte, Fla.: Family Life, 2007.

Zeller, Penny A. *77 Ways Your Family Can Make a Difference: Ideas and Activities for Serving Others.* Kansas City: Beacon Hill, 2008.

ORGANIZATIONS

Apostolate for Family Consecration sponsors Catholic Familyland (for family retreats and catechesis), 3375 County Rd. 36, Bloomingdale, OH 43910-9901; 800-773-2645; www.familyland.org.

Catholics Come Home creates effective and caring messages, broadcast nationally, to encourage Catholics to come home to the Church. P.O. Box 1802, Roswell, GA 30077; CatholicsComeHome.org.

Catholic Grandparents Association helps grandparents share ideas about how to pass on the faith to the next generation. 1171 S. Ocean Blvd., Delray Beach, FL 33483; catholicgrandparentsassociation.wordpress.com.

Catholic Scripture Studies International offers in-depth Scripture study to bring Catholics closer to Jesus Christ and his Church. 9409 Pendennis Ln., Charlotte, NC 28210; 877-228-7830; www.cssprogram.net.

Couple to Couple League is a resource for Natural Family Planning and family-to-family ministry. P.O. Box 111184, Cincinnati, OH 45211-1184; 513-471-2000; www.ccli.org.

Engaged Encounter provides weekend retreats for engaged couples as part of their marriage preparation; www.engagedencounter.org.

Family Missions Company trains missionaries (single or married) for short- and long-term foreign mission work. 12624 Everglade Rd., Abbeville, LA 70510; 337-893-6111; fmcmissions.com.

Fraternus is a ministry to teens that engages the masculine heart and builds virtue through weekly meetings, outdoor excursions, discipleship groups, and summer camp. P.O. Box 840115, St. Augustine, FL 32080; www.fraternus.net.

The Great Adventure Catholic Bible Study (2010) by Jeff Cavins teaches an overview of salvation history. Ascension Press, P.O. Box 1990, West Chester, PA 19380; 800-376-0520; biblestudyforcatholics.com. Materials available for children, too.

The Heritage Foundation is a public policy think tank that promotes principles of free enterprise, limited government, and traditional values. 214 Massachusetts Ave. NE, Washington, D.C. 20002-4999; 202-546-4400. www.heritage.org.

La Leche League offers information on breast-feeding and support groups; www.llli.org.

Lighthouse Catholic Media/NFP provides inspirational CDs and brochures that strengthen our relationship to Christ and his Church. 303 E. State St., Sycamore, IL 60178; 847-488-0333; Lighthousecatholicmedia.org.

One More Soul fosters God's plan for love, marriage, and procreation. 1846 N. Main St., Dayton, OH 45405; 800-307-7685; www.omsoul.com.

Pope Paul VI Institute offers diagnosis and treatment for reproductive disorders. 6901 Mercy Rd., Omaha, NE 68106; 402-390-6600; www.popepaulvi.com.

Pure Freedom helps tweens and teenagers choose purity and modesty. 3006 Research Dr., Suite D-1, State College, PA 16801; 814-234-6072; www.purefreedom.org; www.girlsgonewise.com.

Pure Hope (formerly the National Coalition for the Protection of Children and Families) provides Christian solutions in a sexualized culture, including help for those suffering from addiction to pornography and their families. 800 Compton Rd., Suite 9224, Cincinnati, OH 45231; 513-521-6227; www.purehope.net.

St. Joseph Communications, Inc., is the largest international Catholic audio and video reproduction and distribution company in the United States, providing solid Catholic education on audio CDs and DVDs to families. P.O. Box 729, West Covina, CA 91793; toll-free: 800-526-2151; in California: 626-331-3549; www.saintjoe.com.

St. Joseph's Covenant Keepers is a ministry to families with many helpful resources. Family Life Center, 2130 Wade Hampton Blvd., Greenville, SC 29615; 864-268-6730. www.dads.org.

St. Paul Center for Biblical Theology provides resources for parish-based and online Catholic Scripture studies for laypeople, founded by Scott and Kimberly Hahn. 2228 Sunset Blvd., Suite 2A, Steubenville, OH 43952; 740-264-9535; www.salvationhistory.com.

VIDEO SERIES

Hahn, Kimberly. *Life-Nurturing Love Series* in four installments of six Bible studies each:

> *Chosen and Cherished: Biblical Wisdom for Your Marriage*
> *Graced and Gifted: Biblical Wisdom for the Homemaker's Heart*
> *Beloved and Blessed: Biblical Wisdom for Family Life*
> *Legacy of Love: Biblical Wisdom for Parenting Teens and Young Adults*

For more information contact Servant Books, 800-488-0488; www.servantbooks.org.

NOTES

PART ONE: She Opens Her Hand to the Poor

Chapter One: Personal Compassion for the Poor

1. R. F. Horton, commentary on the book of Proverbs, in W. Robertson Nicoll, ed., *The Expositor's Bible: A Complete Exposition of the Bible* (Hartford, Conn.: S.S. Scranton, 1900), p. 448.

2. John Chrysostom, in Robert Van de Weyer, comp., *On Living Simply: The Golden Voice of John Chrysostom* (Liguori, Mo.: Triumph, 1996), p. 6.

3. Pope Benedict XVI, *Deus Caritas Est,* Encyclical on Christian Love, December 25, 2005, nos. 20, 21, www.vatican.va.

4. Vatican II, *Gaudium et Spes,* Pastoral Constitution on the Church in the Modern World, no. 27, www.vatican.va.

5. José Luis González Balado, ed., *Mother Teresa: In My Own Words* (Liguori, Mo.: Liguori, 1996), p. 23.

6. The St. Paul Center for Biblical Theology provides seminarians with a free collection of books. To donate to this—or to request this for a seminarian you know—contact the St. Paul Center, 2228 Sunset Blvd., Suite 2A, Steubenville, OH 43952; 740-264-9535; www.salvationhistory.com.

Chapter Two: Works of Mercy

1. Philip Howard, *New Every Morning,* p. 95, as quoted in Elisabeth Elliot, *The Shaping of a Christian Family—How My Parents Nurtured My Faith* (Grand Rapids: Revell, 1992), p. 89.

2. Blessed Pope John Paul II, *Gratissimam Sane,* Letter to Families, no. 2, February 22, 1994, www.vatican.va.

3. See Appendix C: Radical Hospitality—An Invitation to Share Life Together.

4. Blessed Pope John Paul II, Letter to Families, no. 10.

5. See www.catholicculture.org.

PART TWO: She Looks Well to the Ways of Her Household

Chapter Three: The Parenting Adventure: Teens

1. Pope Paul VI, Declaration on Christian Education, October 28, 1965, no. 3; www.vatican.va.

2. See Dr. Gary Chapman and Dr. Ross Campbell, *The Five Love Languages of Children* (Chicago: Moody, 1997).

3. Apostolate for Family Consecration, 3375 County Road 36, Bloomingdale, OH 43910-9901; 800-773-2645; www.family-land.org.

4. Blessed Pope John Paul II, *Evangelium Vitae,* Apostolic Letter on the Value and Inviolability of Human Life, March 25, 1995, no. 92, www.vatican.va.

Chapter Four: Nurture Your Teen Toward Maturity

1. See Doran Richards's program "Maidens by His Design," www.BlessingGodsWay.com.

2. For parents and their tweens and teenagers, see www.purefreedom.org and www.girlsgonewise.com.

3. See Kimberly Hahn, *Beloved and Blessed: Biblical Wisdom for Family Life,* Appendix D.

4. This concept is explained very well in Gary and Anne Marie Ezzo, *Reaching the Heart of Your Teen* (Sisters, Oreg.: Multnomah, 1997).

5. Blessed Pope John Paul II, Letter to Families, no. 15.

6. Please contact Pure Hope (formerly the National Coalition for the Protection of Children and Families) for more information, 800 Compton Rd., Suite 9224, Cincinnati, OH 45231; 513-521-667, www.purehope.net.

7. A subscription service for movie reviews and ratings is available at www.screenit.com.

8. See www.purehope.net.

9. Contact Pure Hope to request the "Safe Use Agreement" for cell phones between parents and children.

10. For a novena to Our Lady Undoer of Knots, go to www.theholyrosary.org/maryundoerknots.

PART THREE: She...Does Not Eat the Bread of Idleness

Chapter Five: The Virtue of Friendship

1. Josemaría Escrivá, *Christ Is Passing By* (Princeton, N.J.: Scepter, 1973), p. 9.

2. See Kimberly Hahn, *Beloved and Blessed: Biblical Wisdom for Family Life,* chapters one and two.

3. Randy Alcorn, *The Purity Principle* (Sisters, Oreg.: Multnomah, 2003), p. 55.

4. Shannon Harris, as quoted in Joshua Harris, *Boy Meets Girl: Say Hello to Courtship* (Sisters, Oreg.: Multnomah, 2000), pp. 116–120.

5. Thomas McDonald, "Opting Out of Hooking Up," *The National Catholic Register,* November 1, 2009.

Chapter Six: Preparing Your Teen for the Love of His Life

1. Francis Carvajal, *Lukewarmness: The Devil in Disguise* (Manila: Sinag-Tala, 1978), p. 9.

2. See Josh Harris, *I Kissed Dating Goodbye* (Sisters, Oreg.: Multnomah, 1997), p. 76.

3. Josh McDowell and Dick Day, *Why Wait? What You Need to Know About the Teen Sexuality Crisis* (San Bernardino, Calif.: Here's Life, 1987), p. 79.

4. See Pope Benedict XVI, *Deus Caritas Est,* nos. 3–8.

PART FOUR: Her Children Rise Up and Call Her Blessed

Chapter Seven: Raising Godly Adults in an Ungodly World

1. We have chronicled our story in *Rome Sweet Home: Our Journey to Catholicism* (San Francisco: Ignatius, 1993).

2. See Kimberly Hahn, *Chosen and Cherished: Biblical Wisdom for Your Marriage.*

3. For teaching children on finances, see *Beloved and Blessed: Biblical Wisdom for Family Life.*

Chapter Eight: Honorable Courtship

1. Doug Wilson, *Her Hand in Marriage: Biblical Courtship in the Modern World* (Moscow, Idaho: Canon, 1997), p. 11.

Chapter Nine: Engagement Is a Time of Transition

1. Christopher and Rachel McCluskey, *When Two Become One: Enhancing Sexual Intimacy in Marriage* (Grand Rapids: Revell, 2006).

2. Blessed Pope John Paul II, Letter to Families, no. 14.

3. Annie Chapman, *The Mother-in-Law Dance: Can Two Women Love the Same Man and Still Get Along?* (Eugene, Oreg.: Harvest House, 2004). I highly recommend this book.

PART FIVE: ... Her Husband Also, and He Praises Her

Chapter Eleven: Newlyweds Forge a New Family

1. See *Graced and Gifted* for ideas about liturgical celebrations.

2. St. Elizabeth Ann Seton, as quoted in *The Seton Way,* vol. 11, no. 1 (Winter 2002), p. 2, setonshrine.fnpihost.com.

Chapter Twelve: Consolidating Our Gains as a Growing Family

1. Mike Mason, *The Mystery of Marriage: As Iron Sharpens Iron* (Portland, Oreg.: Multnomah, 1985), p. 138.

2. *Gaudium et Spes,* no. 50, as quoted in the Synod of Bishops, "Christian Family," in Austin Flannery, ed., *Vatican Council II: More Postconciliar Documents,* vol. 2 (Northport, N.Y.: Costello, 1982), p. 857.

3. *Graced and Gifted: Biblical Wisdom for the Homemaker's Heart* is the second volume of the *Life-Nurturing Love* series.

4. A professional interviewer at St. Joseph Communications, Inc., guides you through questions you choose. The result is an edited, state-of-the-art, one-hour recording of your faith journey, giving you twelve copies to share with family and friends and exclusive rights to make more on your own.

5. See catholicgrandparentsassociation.wordpress.com.

PART SIX: A Woman Who Fears the Lord Is to Be Praised

Chapter Thirteen: Witness to the World

1. Blessed Pope John Paul II, Letter to Families, no. 15, www.vatican.va.

2. William Saunders, "The Role of Godparents," *Arlington Catholic Herald,* reprinted at www.catholiceducation.org.

3. See *Code of Canon Law,* 872–874.

4. Blessed Pope John Paul II, *Christifidelis Laici,* Post-Synodal Apostolic Exhortation on the Vocation and the Mission of the Lay Faithful in the Church and in the World, December 30, 1988, no. 3, www.vatican.va.

5. Blessed Pope John Paul II, Letter to Families, no. 16, emphasis in original.

6. The Saint Paul Center, www.salvationhistory.com, offers "Journey through Scripture: Genesis to Jesus," "The Bible and the Mass," "The Bible and the Virgin Mary," and "The Bible and the Sacraments" as online or parish studies.

7. Contact Emmaus Road Publishing for information on Jeff Cavins's and other Scripture studies, 800-398-5470, www.emmausroad.org.

8. Lighthouse Catholic Media/NFP, 303 E. State St., Sycamore, IL 60178; 847-488-0333; Lighthousecatholicmedia.org.

9. Blessed Pope John Paul II, Letter to Families, no. 16.

10. Josemaría Escrivá, *Friends of God* (London: Scepter, 1986), no. 5, p. 3.

11. See CatholicsComeHome.org.

12. Blessed Pope John Paul II, Letter of Endorsement of the Apostolate for Family Consecration, October 10, 1993, www.familyland.org.

Chapter Fourteen: This Is Our Time

1. Blessed Pope John Paul II, Letter to Women, June 29, 1995, no. 10, www.vatican.va.

2. Blessed Pope John Paul II, Letter to Families, no. 17, www.vatican.va.

3. Pope Benedict XVI, *Deus Caritas Est,* no. 28.

4. Blessed Pope John Paul II, Letter to Families, no. 18.

5. Phillip Longman, "Political Victory: From Here to Maternity," *USA Today,* September 2, 2004, p. A23.

6. David Brooks, "The New Red-Diaper Babies," op-ed column, *The New York Times,* December 7, 2004.

7. Pope Benedict XVI, *Deus Caritas Est,* no. 29.

8. Office of the Congregation of the Doctrine of the Faith, "Doctrinal Note Regarding the Participation of Catholics in Political Life," November 24, 2001, no. 1, www.vatican.va.

9. Pope Benedict XVI, *Deus Caritas Est,* no. 28.

10. Pope Paul VI, speech to the United Nations, October 4, 1965, quoted in footnote 24 of Center for Reproductive Law & Policy, "Church or State? The Holy See at the United Nations," www.population-security.org.

11. Blessed Pope John Paul II, Letter to Families, no. 13.

12. Blessed Pope John Paul II, *Redemptoris Missio,* Encyclical on the Permanent Validity of the Church's Missionary Mandate, December 7, 1990, no. 71, www.vatican.va.

13. Blessed Mother Teresa, *Lessons of Love and Secrets of Sanctity,* as quoted in Susan Conroy, "We Are Called to Be Faithful," *Our Sunday Visitor,* www.osv.com.

14. Blessed Pope John Paul II, *Christifidelis Laici,* no. 35.

15. Family Missions Company, 12624 Everglade Rd., Abbeville, LA 70510; 337-893-6111; fmcmissions.com.

Chapter Fifteen: In Praise of Humility

1. Blessed Pope John Paul II, Letter to Families, no. 18, www.vatican.va.

Life-Nurturing Love

building stronger, healthier marriages and families

Legacy of Love
Biblical Wisdom for Parenting Teens and Young Adults

A set of three DVDs featuring Kimberly's warm and inspiring presentation of the *Legacy of Love* material, suitable for personal or group use.

3-DVD set: ISBN 978-1-61636-001-6 | $29.99

Available at www.ServantBooks.org.

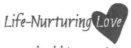

building stronger, healthier marriages and families

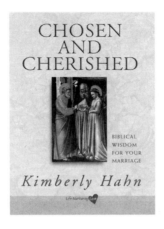

Chosen and Cherished
Biblical Wisdom for Your Marriage

The first book in the *Life-Nurturing Love* series offers tools to help you build your marriage on the firm foundation of faith. Applying Sacred Scripture, Church teaching, and practical wisdom, Kimberly Hahn helps you explore:

- Conflict resolution in your marriage
- Communication skills with your spouse
- Setting shared financial goals
- Healing wounds of unfaithfulness
- Cultivating a spirit of generosity toward your spouse

Book: ISBN 978-0-86716-848-8 | $14.99 | Also on DVD!
3-DVD set: ISBN 978-1-61636-118-1 | $29.99

Available at www.ServantBooks.org.

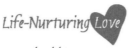

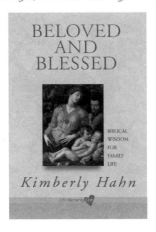

About the Author

KIMBERLY HAHN is the author of *Chosen and Cherished: Biblical Wisdom for Your Marriage; Graced and Gifted: Biblical Wisdom for the Homemaker's Heart; Beloved and Blessed: Biblical Wisdom for Family Life;* and *Life-Giving Love: Embracing God's Beautiful Design for Marriage.* She is the coauthor, with her husband, Scott, of *Rome Sweet Home: Our Journey to Catholicism.* Kimberly is the mother of six children and is a frequent conference speaker on topics related to marriage and family life.